CONFESSIONS OF AN HABITUAL ADMINISTRATOR

Confessions of an Habitual Administrator
An Academic Survival Manual

PAUL T. BRYANT

ANKER PUBLISHING COMPANY, INC.
Bolton, Massachusetts

Confessions of an Habitual Administrator
An Academic Survival Manual

ISBN 1-882982-86-X

Composition by Beverly Jorgensen, Studio J Graphic Design
Cover design by Jennifer Arbaiza Graphic Design

Anker Publishing Company, Inc.
563 Main Street
P.O. Box 249
Bolton, MA 01740-0249 USA

www.ankerpub.com

Library of Congress Cataloging-in-Publication Data

Bryant, Paul T.
    Confessions of an habitual administrator : an academic survival manual /
Paul T. Bryant.
        p. cm.
    Includes index.
    ISBN 1-882982-86-X
    1. College administrators—United States. I. Title.

    LB2341.B714 2005
    378.1'11—dc22
                                        2004030344

To Genny, Elaine, and Chris, who bore with me,

and

To the many dedicated, hardworking faculty and students for whom good administrative work should be done and who make such work worthwhile.

Many shall run to and fro, and knowledge shall be increased.

—Book of Daniel 12:4

ABOUT THE AUTHOR

Paul T. Bryant attended four colleges and universities, earning B.S. and M.S. degrees in botany and M.A. and Ph.D. degrees in English. This background led to a scholarly interest in nature writing and environmental literature. As a faculty member, he served at four colleges and universities, holding every academic rank from instructor through full professor. As an administrator, he held positions of editor, director, assistant department chair, department chair, assistant dean, associate dean, and dean. As an editor, he worked with faculty and administrators at colleges and universities across the United States, visiting many of their campuses. His career spans 46 years in academe.

TABLE OF CONTENTS

PREFACE

This book is not intended to provide a comprehensive system for establishing the perfect administrative structure for a university or any other organization. It does not offer a system title containing power words like "quality" or "strategic" or "objectives." Comprehensive systems, because they try to fit all cases, seldom fit any specific case well. Indeed, too often implementing such a system will soak up too much time and energy that should have been devoted to running the university. An actual, individual administrator has to deal with a single, specific organization, its particular set of circumstances, its individual people, its peculiar assets and liabilities, day by day.

For such real, live, nontheoretical administrators, and for the people affected by their work, I present the lessons I have learned in 46 years of academic experience, the majority of them in various administrative positions. I have found these lessons relevant in a variety of settings. I have distilled these lessons into some general rules, which I frivolously call "Bryant's Laws." Like most laws, they must be applied with judgment and will be found to have exceptions. Their application suggests that time-honored ROTC response to a tactical question: "Sir! It depends on the situation and the terrain." Much as we might find comfort in absolutes, good administration relies on good judgment at the moment. Rules, systems, "laws," are only useful as guidelines and warning signs. A good administrator will always take into account the situation and the terrain.

Universities change administrative structures and procedures from time to time. Some seem to be changing them constantly. Nevertheless, human nature remains constant. The human foibles that my colleagues and I exhibited in the experiences I relate are still in play on college and university campuses across the country. These foibles are not the fault of the university. They arise from human nature. Variations of them can be found in any human organization, whether it be school, church, small business, large corporation, farm, ranch, government bureau, or nonprofit philanthropic foundation. They may take slightly different forms depending upon their setting, but they all arise from the same basic human nature, a nature we cannot escape.

On this basis, I offer some practical principles for survival, anchored, I hope, on a clear concept of what a university should strive to be. I will illustrate these principles with examples drawn from my own experience as student, staff member, faculty member, and administrator at seven universities.

On the subject of human foibles, I should point out that this account, like all more or less biographical accounts, will tend to emphasize the positive. Those times when I was inept, mistaken, or a downright fool, frequent as they may have been, will seem to have faded from my memory. Those times when I seem to have behaved more or less properly will come to the fore. Furthermore, those with whom I found myself in disagreement on the occasions I relate here would likely have strikingly different accounts of what happened and why. I offer my perception and recollection as accurately as I can. What can you expect? Even administrators are human, if only by a very narrow margin.

ACKNOWLEDGMENTS

My special thanks to Dean David Penniman and to my ever-patient wife, Genevieve Dale Bryant, for their careful reading and good advice. They have no responsibility for any errors or foolishness contained herein, but they deserve credit for reducing the frequency of such things.

PROLOGUE

> *Upon the education of the people of this country the fate*
> *of the country depends.*
>
> —Benjamin Disraeli

American colleges and universities represent one of the truly grand achievements of our civilization. They are at once the conservators of our past and major agents in shaping our future.

As conservators, they preserve and transmit to following generations our history (and the lessons it should teach us), our traditions, and all the knowledge of ourselves and our world that we have achieved up to the present moment. In this role, one might expect universities to be bastions of the status quo, stultifyingly fixed in a carefully formulated past that admits of no revision. The aged professor with his yellowing lecture notes unchanged since he left graduate school might represent the worst form of such conservatism. The brilliant teacher who introduces students to the lessons of our history and to our rich heritage of art, literature, science, and philosophy might represent the best.

Simultaneously with the university's conservative role, research for new knowledge and the constant reexamination of what we think we already know make American universities perhaps the greatest agency of organized, deliberate change in the history of humanity. Given the limits of human knowledge, effective research makes change inevitable. American universities regard continuing research and creative activity as a part of their basic function. Thus, in addition to passing on to students our cultural and intellectual heritage, the university faculty continue to add to our knowledge and, ideally, give the next generation of scholars the intellectual tools, and the motivation, to add again to that heritage through research. Change, then, is continuously, generation after generation, programmed into our culture through the students coming out of our universities and the faculty who teach them.

A major university campus presents a dazzling aggregation of people who know things. The campus contains people who are knowledgeable, even expert, in almost every area of human knowledge and inquiry. Whether the question is the etymology of an obscure word or the etiology of a fatal disease, solutions to industrial pollution or insight into the nature of Jupiter's moons, a university campus is a primary place to seek an answer. A student at a major university has access to more people with greater expertise about more things than most people will likely ever see again in an entire lifetime. Unfortunately, few students appreciate the intellectual and cultural opportunities a university offers them. For the few who do understand the wealth of knowledge (and so of power) available to them, the universe is almost literally spread before them to study, to explore, to experience, and finally to change. Not many other institutions in our society can offer so much.

Beyond its challenging and complex role as reservoir, generator, and transmitter of all aspects of human knowledge, experience, and accomplishment, the average American university undertakes to provide a wide range of social and cultural services to the faculty and students, to the local and regional communities, and to the general public. Universities harbor and support creative artists, creative researchers, and creative thinkers of all sorts. They offer a venue for the public performance of all the arts—music, drama, and the graphic arts, for example. They provide a forum for the debate of ideas, whether political, religious, social, economic, philosophical, artistic, or scientific. They are home to university presses and professional journals of many kinds. Their libraries amass collections of our printed (and, increasingly, electronically preserved) records of our knowledge, experience, and thought, preserving manuscripts, rare books, photographs, maps, even works of art, that might otherwise not have survived.

Universities act as gatekeepers to the critical professions, assuring through their credentialing that our physicians, attorneys, teachers, engineers, psychologists, counselors, and other practitioners have the basic knowledge to qualify them for their practice.

Along with a feast of human knowledge, universities make available to students an impressive array of counseling, advising, and other support services. In loco parentis has in many ways disappeared from the campus scene, at least in the form of curfew and other such rules. But as the university has fewer rules controlling a student's social life, it has taken more responsibility for the student's intellectual life. There was a time when a student was expected to sink or swim academically on the basis of his or her own efforts and ability, perhaps with some guidance from a faculty advisor. Now students have a whole array of tutoring, counseling, advising, and testing services practically forced upon them, particularly if they get into academic difficulties. Without setting or enforcing many rules, the university nevertheless takes an interest in, and provides assistance and support for, a student's social life, mental health, physical health, career aspirations, and, as graduation approaches, search for employment.

Credentialing has become an increasingly important function. The student who comes to the university, studies certain subjects, and is able to demonstrate a required level of command of those subjects, is publicly given credentials certifying the judgment of the university faculty that the student has achieved the specified knowledge. The credentialing may come in the form of credit hours in certain courses, certificates of completion of short courses of study, or most importantly, degrees, which range from the baccalaureate through specialized or general master's degrees to various doctorates. These judgments are made by the university faculty, and they must be recorded and preserved permanently by the university registrar. These credentials have come to carry very substantial value in our complex society as indicators of knowledge and ability. In effect, the society that created and supports the university relies upon the university's credentialing function in many of our business, economic, technical, legal, social, and medical decisions. It is a responsibility that the university should not take lightly. Course content should be complete and present the best, most current knowledge. Requirements should be rigorous, and grades and credits should be awarded carefully and responsibly. Professors publicly put their professional judgments on the line when awarding grades and credits, and society is, in many ways, putting itself at the mercy of those judgments.

Particularly since the mid-20th century, our society has looked to universities for both basic and applied research in virtually every field of human knowledge. The generation of new knowledge has become an established role for American universities, making them an agent of planned change. This research is supported by the university's regular operating budget, and even more by special grants and contracts from government agencies, professional associations, private foundations, and corporations. These funds, which can total in the tens of millions of dollars at major research universities, must be solicited in often elaborate proposals. They must then be accounted for and expended for a dazzling complex of sophisticated equipment, faculty time, research assistants, and the substantial indirect costs associated with maintaining a research effort. Understandably, the sources of the funding expect to receive regular reports of progress and final detailed reports upon completion of the work. Once the research is completed, the usual expectation is that the results will be published in the professional literature of the field. The prompt and accurate communication of research findings has become a major consumer of time and effort.

All of these activities must be supported by such essential core facilities as a library and computer systems. Developing and maintaining a major research library, keeping it current and accessible, and protecting and preserving existing collections is a complex and difficult enterprise. Developing and maintaining computer systems for storage and retrieval of records, and for myriad research functions, can challenge a considerable staff of able technical people as well as the faculty and administrators who use the systems.

All of these various activities have to take place somewhere. The modern classroom, with its audiovisual and information processing sophistication, has become much more than a simple room with chairs, a podium, and a chalkboard. The teaching laboratory becomes even more complex with its provisions for student experiments and the necessary measures for student safety. Research laboratories can be the most complex and specialized of all, sometimes requiring not only special environmental controls and lighting, but also special electronic and electrical power resources, ventilation, shielding, and so on. Someone has to identify these physical needs, plan the structures, oversee their construction, and maintain them.

With all of these functions, and their considerable economic, social, and cultural consequences, American universities have grown into complex and sophisticated organizations. Their sources of funding are as varied as their responsibilities. Someone has to tend to all of these functions to allow the individual faculty member to focus on his or her own classes, students, and research. The people who do so are called administrators. Despite the negative attitudes toward them that is traditionally maintained by many faculty (more on that later), universities, and their faculties, could not function without them. The faculty member who claims self-sufficiency and independence of the university structure (and I have encountered those who do), naively takes for granted all those things that are provided at the cost of a great deal of time, effort, and money.

The great hazard for American universities today is the same trap that faces any large, complex, well-established organization that has existed with a reasonable level of success and approval for an extended period of time. An entrenched institution may eventually begin to focus more on its own well-being and survival than on the mission(s) for which it was originally established and which society continues to support. When that happens, the institution's continued existence is in jeopardy, although the threat may be slow in developing. When it does develop, either substantial reform or annihilation will result.

Something like that situation occurred for universities in the 1960s and 1970s, and some reform did come about. Unfortunately, many of the would-be reformers overreached and botched the job of reform. They were so strident and deliberately outrageous that they made enemies of those they needed as friends—a serious error.

Another error was the would-be reformers' assumption that reform could occur in two separate stages. The first stage was the destruction, willy-nilly, of currently existing educational structures. The second stage, to come only after the first was completed, was to develop a radically new system for higher education. When asked what their new regime would be, they could not answer. In effect, they said that once control was in their hands, they would decide what the new system would be. Very few outside their movement were willing to buy that pig in a poke.

Perhaps the would-be reformers' most fundamental error was the assumption that all those in any position of responsibility or influence were, by virtue of that fact, selfish, shortsighted, and generally evil. Equally, they assumed that those with no responsibility or influence were selfless, wise, and concerned only for the greater good. Both such sweeping, categorical assumptions were so obviously contradicted by experience that the radical reformers eventually lost all credibility.

Finally, lacking understanding of how a university community works, they made demands that the majority of students saw as destructive. In their absolutism they overreached and created a backlash that hindered genuine reform. They also winnowed the ranks of administrators, eliminating the timid and uncertain, and leaving a cadre of shrewd, tough-minded people who could not be pushed around. In difficult times, under pressure, a Darwinian form of natural selection can take place among academic administrators. Those who survive may become highly resistant strains.

The usual follies of human nature were operating then and continue to operate now. We can learn from our own and our universities' past. Each generation should have some liberty to make its own mistakes and not simply repeat those of previous generations.

1 How Professors Become Administrators, or, Where Did We Go Wrong?

> *Government is a contrivance of human wisdom to provide for human wants. Men have a right that these wants should be provided for by this wisdom.*
>
> —Edmund Burke

The Alternative Path

An effective academic administrator must be a kind of intellectual amphibian, one who is qualified, competent, and experienced as a teacher and researcher, but at the same time one who has an array of skills not required of the average faculty member. These include such basic matters as being able to read and understand budget documents and manage complex budgets, and such less definable matters as communication skills, a practical sense of human nature, patience, judgment, ability to plan and organize, and other capabilities often grouped under the heading of "leadership." Some acquaintance with the law can also be useful.

Probably very few academics begin their career with the conscious intention of becoming an administrator. There may be a few—those in business administration, perhaps, or other administratively oriented fields—but most of us had a romantic view of ourselves as kindly old Professor Warmheart, in Harris tweed jacket with leather elbow patches, strolling leisurely under the arching campus elms, puffing his beloved briar, followed by admiring undergraduates who hang upon his every word. Or as the clear-eyed, steely minded young scientist or philosopher or critic, seeking truth, cutting through the cant, prejudice, and obfuscation of our elders to set the intellectual world on the right track at last, again followed by students eager for a higher plane of knowledge.

Unfortunately, eager and admiring students are in short supply on most campuses these days. So most of us settle for a life of competent teaching of such students as come to our classes. Some of us may also try to further our field of knowledge through research and publication. Those who aspire to fame and fortune are more likely to take the path of research and publication than of administration, and they are well advised to do so. Administrators may be generally known on their own campus, but seldom do any other than presidents become known beyond their own institution.

So how and why do some of us get into the administrative predicament? It's not enough to say that it's a hard job but somebody has to do it. That is true enough, but not the whole story.

Circumstances are as varied as the people caught up in them. In some cases the academic scene was so muddled that the choice was to get it straightened out or leave, and no one else was willing to take on the job. Perhaps the other candidates for the job were so awful that he or she took it on in self-defense. Maybe the salary increase of a 12-month appointment looked good as the children at home approached college age. (The monthly salary of department chairs and even of deans does not always match the salaries of the more highly paid full professors. This makes the economic motive uncertain in many cases.)

The reason for joining the administrative ranks may be more complex. If a full professor becomes disenchanted with the situation at his or her institution, accepting an administrative position elsewhere may be the only way to move. Senior faculty who are not nationally known scholars find it very difficult to move, except to administrative positions. When a department has faculty positions to fill, most prefer to bring in young, entry-level instructors or assistant professors (at entry-level salaries), rather than more expensive senior people. Then, too, the senior people may expect instant tenure, whereas the department has a few years before making such a commitment to the new assistant professor.

Various of these and other reasons operated in my long and checkered career. Over the years I have held every academic rank from instructor through full professor. Administratively, at four different institutions, I have been assistant editor, editor, director, assistant department chair, acting department chair, department chair, assistant dean, associate dean, acting dean, and dean. I was encouraged on various occasions to apply for vice presidencies, but resisted the idea successfully. Hence my views and experience in academic administration are those of middle management, the people involved in the day-to-day operation of the institution.

Free Advice and Probably Worth the Cost

In view of this experience, I have been asked for advice from time to time by younger colleagues who have been offered administrative positions. Early in my administrative experience I formulated:

BRYANT'S FIRST LAW OF ACADEMIC ADMINISTRATION

No one should have an administrative position who wants it.

Such a draconian law is, of course, an overstatement. There are good administrators who have willingly accepted, even sought, their positions. The hyperbole is intended to emphasize a point.

My reasoning was that anyone who actually wants an administrative position may want it for the wrong reasons—either a misconception of what the job is or a desire for power and prestige (which amounts to a misconception of the job). Many faculty have an exaggerated view of the benefits of administrative positions. The economic benefits are only marginally if at all significant. Comparing the 12-month salary of an administrator with the 9-month salary of a faculty member (without adding summer school salaries) is deceptive. Salaries should be compared on a monthly basis. As for the supposed power of an administrative position, almost any decision an administrator makes is hemmed in by constraints of all kinds: budget limits, limits on positions, university regulations established by governing boards, higher administration, or faculty councils and committees, as well as basic considerations of what the faculty, students, and higher administration will support. Initiating a new program or policy without the approval and support of the faculty, for example, is an exercise in sheer futility. Finally, such latitude as the administrator does have for making decisions will seldom allow for any decision that directly benefits the administrator. Anyone accepting an administrative position for the sake of power is in for frustration and disappointment, and may even deserve it.

A second element behind this "First Law" is that an administrator who actually wants the job may be more likely to compromise principles for the sake of keeping the job. An administrator who really does not care about the job will be more likely to maintain his or her personal integrity in making a tough decision. "If the vice president doesn't like my decision, he can fire me and get someone else to do his dirty work," can be a healthy attitude if not overdone. Of course, constantly balancing on a hair trigger, regularly threatening to resign if you do not get your way, is childish and annoying, but in a major crisis of integrity for the unit or the university, it can be liberating to act without worrying whether or not your action will get you fired.

As might be expected, the First Law seemed too sweeping for my colleagues, so I fell back on:

BRYANT'S SECOND LAW OF ACADEMIC ADMINISTRATION

Always be aware that a university has no memory
and no conscience.

If you can live comfortably with that characteristic of universities, you might find administration interesting, and perhaps even rewarding. If you cannot accept it, but still choose to become an administrator, the university will eventually break your heart.

The university's lack of memory or conscience is, of course, a function of the people there, and the way universities are run. Decision-makers, particularly in the impersonal context of a committee, may neither know nor care about any previous behavior or any previous commitments made by others.

For example, years of faithful and effective service to a university will carry no weight with a selection committee or a president seeking to fill an administrative position. They will base their decisions on whether or not the candidate will serve what they (sometimes erroneously) believe to be their best interests. A candidate who shows any sign of putting principle before their interests may be out of the running. Sometimes this works especially against internal candidates because they already know where the bodies are buried and what scams are being operated. They may also know about those awkward earlier commitments and obligations. By the same token, a selection committee may know, or think it knows, how an internal candidate will perform and what principles she or he will act upon. It often may seem safer to bring in the outsider who is not so well informed and who shows signs of being amenable to the committee's views. In any case, we all know the old saw about an expert being someone from out of town.

It is true that individual administrators, and individual members of policymaking committees, have consciences, and some will heed them. But unless they are unusually persuasive, courageous, and tenacious, they will likely be pushed aside by the impersonality of the decision-making process. This is not peculiar to universities. It is characteristic of any large organization, be it corporate, governmental, educational, or military. Ironically, the more broadly democratic the process, the more impersonal it is likely to be.

Personal Costs

If, on the other hand, the internal candidate is selected (usually the internal candidate comes at a lower cost), he or she, once in the position, will find that past associations, friendships, favors, good deeds, integrity of behavior, or other exemplary characteristics, have no influence on his or her status. It is as if the administrator, by entering such a position, has been reborn with no past history. Trusted as a colleague before, the new administrator is suddenly suspect in any action or decision.

This change in status was driven home for me when I first became the acting chair of my department. I had served as assistant to the previous department chair, as a favor to help him at his request. When he abruptly resigned in the middle of a semester, the dean and various members of the department put enormous pressure on me to serve as acting chair. Given the turmoil in the department at that time, I very much did not want to have to grapple with its problems. Finally, after two high-pressure meetings with the dean, and with the perhaps foolish belief that I might be able to hold the departmental situation together until a new chair could be found, I reluctantly agreed.

No sooner had the news of my acceptance gotten around than one of my better friends in the department stopped by to tell me I had his support. I was pleased to know that, until his final observation. He said that of course anyone who takes on an administrative job does so for the power and thenceforth is not to be trusted. He wanted me to know that he realized that, but thought I might be marginally better than the average. I protested that I had no interest in power (I don't even like to give a student a final grade). I was taking the job to try to help the department, which was in considerable disarray, and which was losing credibility with the rest of the university. He would hear none of it. He was convinced I wanted to exercise power and that administrators are not to be trusted. I had clearly fallen from the ranks of the blessed. This taint may even carry beyond an individual's time of administrative service. I recall an occasion when a faculty council was debating the acceptance of a revised procedure for faculty grievances. The proposed new system had been developed by an elected committee of the faculty. A group of faculty made an impassioned plea against adopting the new system purely on the ground that it had been developed by a committee that included two former department chairs! Apparently the mark of Cain was still on their brows. I should add that the majority of the council voted to adopt the new system.

This sudden change of status reaches into personal as well as "official" relationships. For example, when participating in easy banter as a colleague, the new administrator must suddenly be careful of the most joking remark because it is perceived as having administrative power behind it and just might be serious. The only acceptable humor from an administrator is that which is self-deprecating. Anything else is threatening, a veiled wielding of power. The amusing dry wit of a colleague has, with that colleague's assumption of administrative responsibility, become ominous, indirect coercion.

Mr. Hyde has suddenly emerged from kindly old Dr. Jeckyll's laboratory. The Second Law is in full effect: no memory and no conscience.

The Professional Cost

If the professor, by turning administrator, gains some enhanced ability to influence the working of the university, what beyond personal relationships is lost? Professionally, as a teacher and scholar/researcher, there are also losses. Sometimes a prominent professor is placed as a figurehead in an administrative position to enhance the prestige of the institution. Such a "star" will often be given assistants to actually do the administrative work. And once in a great while there is that gifted individual who can continue to do prolific research, publish prestigiously, occasionally teach a class brilliantly, and still fill a real administrative post effectively, but those are rare. Most administrative positions, if taken seriously and responsibly, require hard work, time, and energy that cannot then be spent on preparing to teach or on research and publication. Just finding time to read the journals and stay current in an academic field can become a challenge.

One solution to this problem, a solution pursued by a good many administrators, is to let administrative responsibilities go untended instead of taking them seriously. I recall hearing a presentation by a graduate dean of a major state university. He was to explain, for the benefit of other deans, how he had solved a major administrative problem at his institution. The rest of us were expected to benefit from his tutoring.

The problem, which had begun to develop at least months and probably years earlier, was a major backlog of applications for graduate admission. His office had normally assembled the application materials, checked them for completeness, reviewed them against the university's basic graduate admission requirements (undergraduate degree, grade point average, standardized test scores, and so on), and then referred the completed application file to the individual departments for a final decision. The fact that a huge backlog of applications had developed over a period of time, without the dean becoming aware of it sooner, suggested that the dean was not involved in the day-to-day functioning of his office. But once the problem was called to his attention as a crisis, he quickly developed a solution. His solution was to hand all of those troublesome processing chores over to the individual departments (without reducing his own staff or increasing theirs). When an application came in, it was sent, unchecked, to the relevant department. A neat solution to any administrative problem, apparently, is to give that problem to someone else to solve. Pass the buck.

On the other hand, an administrator who takes the job seriously (responsibly) will find it necessary to invest significant time and energy in doing it. The result, of course, is that the administrator is on a diverging professional path from the professor. To pursue our earlier metaphor, the amphibious administrator will be increasingly out of the swim and stranded on dry land.

An administrator should continue to teach and to do research, if only to be reminded regularly of the trials and tribulations of the faculty day by day, and to keep in mind what the university is there for. Such activities also give the administrator some slight credibility with the faculty. But it is not possible to maintain the same level of intensity and productivity as a full-time teacher and scholar. Year by year, that difference becomes wider in total productivity, until finally it is very difficult to go back to the other career. For young faculty members considering the administrative route, I suggest they first wait until they are tenured, and then that they not commit to more than a year, or two at most, at the outset. One year out of an academic career can be made up, perhaps two, if the administrative life does not seem congenial. Five years and the gap begins to be very wide.

Becoming an Administrator

If, with these caveats in mind, the young faculty member still would like to explore the administrative path, how should he or she go about it? One way is to be organized, well informed (not just gossip), and responsible in faculty governance. Be willing to serve on a reasonable number of faculty committees. When serving on committees, attend meetings regularly, carry out assigned tasks faithfully and on time, understand how faculty governance works, and participate in helpful, positive ways in faculty deliberations. A good friend (an organizational psychologist) once told me that if you want to be made chair of a new committee, come to the first committee meeting with a clipboard. Show, in other words, that you are organized and prepared to keep track of what the committee is doing. In essence, that is the idea. Such behavior will make a faculty member's name pop up when administrative assignments are being considered. Stability, responsibility, and good sense are sometimes valued, even at universities.

2 THE SELECTION PROCESS

*But where shall wisdom be found? and where is the
place of understanding?*
—Book of Esther 28:12

There was a time when many administrators were simply appointed by the president, vice president, or, for a department head or
chair, by a dean. This has become less common, or at least the appearance of such arbitrary selection is less common. Sometimes a department chair has been elected by the department faculty from among its
existing members. More often the process begins with the selection of
a faculty committee, the "search committee." The dynamics of such a
committee are usually intricate and definitive for the outcome of its
deliberations.

The Search Committee

The committee may be appointed by the vice president/provost or
other officer, or it may be elected by the faculty group for whom the
administrator is being sought.

If administratively appointed, its membership will be carefully selected to assure that certain viewpoints will prevail. This can be done
by careful knowledge of individuals or by patterns of representation.

For example, if both a dean and a department chair of the same college are appointed, it is likely that there will be two votes for that dean's viewpoint. On the other hand, a shrewd administrator may appoint a faculty radical, a gadfly, to the committee, to show that all views are being represented. When this is the case, you may suspect that there are enough "safe" votes on the committee to see that the gadfly does not prevail. The negative aspect of the appointment method is that it is subject to such manipulation. The positive aspect is that by including administrators in the mix, the committee may have some judgment of what the administrative position entails and what characteristics and experience are useful in filling it. The selection of any appointed committee can be a delicate art. Obviously, the outcome of a committee's deliberations is to a considerable extent determined by the makeup of the committee.

If an appointed committee seems to be a hodgepodge casually chosen and to include a high number of ineffective or cantankerous members, the work of the committee probably will not be taken seriously. Such a committee is intended only as a way to delay an issue, or is not expected to agree on any recommendation, or may produce recommendations so patently ridiculous that they can be safely ignored. Or it may be administrative response to complaints by the ineffective faculty that they never get put on committees. In that case such a committee is merely a sop to the Cerberus of faculty demands for input.

If the faculty appointed to the committee include highly respected and effective professors who are frequently elected by the faculty to represent them, then the administration probably plans to take the committee's recommendations seriously.

If the faculty elect some or all members of a selection committee, other problems, and other advantages, result. On the positive side, the membership of the committee should represent the views of the faculty, if the faculty as a group took the trouble to vote and to consider carefully the effects of their voting. As with any other democratic process, this may not always be the case. An example of the problem of faculty awareness once occurred for me when a department with a weak graduate program regularly elected a certain senior professor to represent the department on the graduate council. This professor loudly and vigorously opposed having any graduate program at all. In view of this and of his perennial presence on the graduate council, I asked the department chair if his faculty would prefer to abandon their graduate program. I had long before learned that no program will be any good unless the faculty involved support it. The department chair assured me that the faculty wanted their graduate program. Why then, I asked, do they send such an outspoken opponent of the program to represent them? The only answer I could get was that this was a senior professor who had always been on the graduate council. The departmental faculty could not bring themselves to make a change.

This, of course, was an extreme case. Usually, elected committees have a majority of strong members. The recommendations of such committees have a reasonable hope, though not an assurance, of general faculty support. With strong faculty support and careful deliberation behind them, the recommendations of such a committee are likely to be accepted.

Ways and Means

On the negative side, most faculty members, including those on selection committees, have no real concept of what administrative positions entail. In broad terms, most faculty have little sense of what I would call "ways and means." To illustrate, consider this: On any given weekday during a university's school year, hundreds of faculty will be meeting with thousands of students in classes dealing with topics that very nearly run the gamut of human knowledge. In each instance, a teacher knowledgeable on the specific subject, and prepared to teach it, meets in a specified place at a specified time with a group of students who either wish to know more about the subject or are required to know more by their curriculum. They will meet in a furnished and equipped classroom or laboratory. The room will have been cleaned and reasonably maintained. The electric lights will come on when the switch is flipped. The heating or air conditioning system will maintain an acceptable temperature. A record will have been made of the enrollment of these particular students in this particular course, and at the end a record will be made and preserved of their individual performance in the course. The room in which the group meets will be in a building that was probably planned for this use, and designed and constructed and maintained with such classes in mind. All of this requires a good deal of money, a lot of planning, and a lot of work by many people. But the average faculty member takes it all for granted, gives it no thought, unless of course something goes wrong. If two classes are scheduled for the same room at the same time, or if the professor is in English and the class is in chemistry, then there is faculty complaint about the idiots in administration. Otherwise, the whole complex process is invisible to most faculty. They may see no reason why anyone should be asked to teach a class at 8 a.m. ("I'm just not a morning person."). Such faculty, and a good many students, feel that the university ought to find the millions needed to build enough classrooms and laboratories, and hire enough faculty, so that all classes can be offered between 10:00 a.m. and 3:00 p.m. But they see no reason why they and their students should not all arrive at a suitable place at the same time, ready for teaching and for learning. They give little thought to ways and means.

I recall a meeting with a faculty group who were demanding more money for some particular activity that they felt, quite rightly, was very important. Their expectations for increased funding were substantial. As we discussed it with them ("we" were a dean, an associate dean, and a couple of department chairs), we were trying to see where in the budget we could find such funds. The concept we were having trouble communicating was that we did not have an infinite amount of money available, that if we gave their project more money, we would have less money for something else. All of our budget was committed. The problem was finding an activity from which we could justifiably take money away.

Trying to convey this concept, I made the mistake of saying, "You have to realize that this is a zero-sum game." The senior faculty member to whom I said this exploded in my face. "This is not a game!" he shouted. "That's the trouble with you administrators, you think this is just a game. This is serious!" And so on.

After his explosion had subsided, I assured him that I shared his view that this was a serious matter, and tried again to explain what I meant by my comment. I think he finally understood, but I was never sure that he did.

W. L. Everitt, longtime and highly respected dean of engineering at the University of Illinois, once told me that faculty members typically believe that their department chair has a secret fund that can finance anything the chair wants to support. The dean said he could assure me that his department chairs had no such fund. The chairs, in turn, he said, believed that the dean had such a secret fund. He assured me that was not the case. However, he said, he thought the provost probably had one. My "zero-sum" conversation was, I suppose, an example of that "secret fund" myth.

Professors and Administrators

Because so many faculty members have little sense of ways and means, and even less understanding of the requirements of an administrative position, the candidates for an administrative position who will be favored by the average faculty committee will not necessarily be the best administrators. Faculty committees tend to favor candidates who demonstrate the qualities of strong faculty members. Prestigious publications and large research grants in particular attract favorable notice. Strong teaching skills may attract some notice, but teaching excellence is often harder to document or evaluate. Years ago it became the practice in the sciences to list the doctoral programs successfully directed as part of a candidate's curriculum vitae, almost as if one were setting one's lance up outside one's lodge, with all the scalps one has taken on display on the shaft of the lance. Successful doctorates are admirable accomplishments and may demonstrate that a candidate is intelligent and hardworking, and would be a valuable addition to the faculty, but they do not necessarily demonstrate administrative ability or even a willingness to do administrative work.

Unfortunately, some universities, even prestigious ones, have descended to the level of awarding doctorates to any graduate student who serves adequately as a research assistant for a number of years. Such individuals may be skilled in only one laboratory technique (e.g., running a cell sorter or a spectrograph) and may not have the breadth and depth of knowledge usually associated with the Ph.D. After all, Ph.D. is supposed to stand for "Doctor of Philosophy," not "Doctor of a Single Technology." It should signify a broad grasp of the major field and some understanding of at least one or two related fields, as well as some awareness of the underlying philosophical assumptions that drive the field. Directing the programs of pseudo-doctorates that involve only work on a specific project could hardly be regarded as a significant accomplishment. In fact, it may call the director's academic integrity into question. Such people may not be effective academic administrators, though they may come from supposedly first-line universities. Unfortunately, these biases of most faculty toward qualities that they admire in faculty may lead to choices of administrators with no aptitude for administration.

These biases may also lead to choices of administrators who have no interest in actually doing the work of administration. Let me give an example. As the new chair of a large department, I needed someone from the faculty to act as coordinator of the graduate program. This meant chairing the department's graduate committee, overseeing admissions to the departmental graduate program, and with the graduate committee, establishing and maintaining graduate standards and requirements. The position carried a reduced teaching load, in recognition of the demands of these various duties. I went to a senior professor whose publications were the most impressive in the department, and whose academic standards in his own classes were known to be high. I discussed with him the duties of the position and the reduced teaching load. He agreed to serve. I was pleased.

A week or so later, I took to our new graduate coordinator a stack of applications for admission to our graduate program. The usual procedure had been for the graduate coordinator to run through the applications quickly, eliminating those candidates who obviously did not meet our requirements for admission, and then passing the rest of the folders around to the members of the graduate committee. The committee would then meet and vote on each application, to admit or deny. With a little practice, most folders could be examined very quickly and passed on.

The graduate coordinator was not in his office, but his door was open, so I left the applications on his desk with a note. Minutes later he was in my office, holding the pile of applications and demanding to know what I expected him to do with all that. I explained again, as I had on the day he agreed to serve, how the admission review process worked. Without further ado, he announced that he did not have time to bother with such red tape, put the applications on my desk (already crowded with other red tape), and resigned as graduate coordinator. Apparently he liked the prestige of being graduate coordinator and the relief of a reduced teaching load, but had no patience for actually doing any of the work. That is sometimes the problem with candidates favored by faculty search committees.

I recall similar problems with candidates for a graduate deanship. The selection committee was much impressed by candidates who had been very successful at gaining large government research grants. The committee invited two such candidates to our campus for extended interviews. I was assigned the task of hosting a substantial part of their interview visits. As these visits proceeded, it became quite obvious to me that these candidates had little interest in graduate students, except to the extent that they could serve as low-paid research assistants. When I arranged for them to meet with the graduate office staff—the people who did the bulk of the work of the graduate school, and who did it extraordinarily well—both candidates made it abundantly clear that they had no interest in them or in their work. Not to display even simple courtesy toward the people who will run your administrative operation is either to have an administrative death wish or to lack all sense of the responsibilities of the deanship. Yet the selection committee was mightily impressed by both candidates. Fortunately for that graduate school, the vice president and the president were not so impressed. Both candidates might have been very strong additions to the research faculty, but they would not have been effective as administrators.

This is not to say that upper administrators are infallible in their choices of candidates. Sometimes they can be, well, idiosyncratic at the least. For example, on one occasion a group of deans was asked to interview candidates for a directorship. After the deans met with the first candidate, they gathered to discuss their reactions to him. They considered all aspects of his candidacy carefully. His experience was good, but his phlegmatic personality did not bode well for a position that required working extensively with students. The deans concluded they could not recommend the candidate. When they next met with the vice president responsible for making the final selection, they worked patiently through other agenda items, then brought up the question of the candidate. At that point, before the deans could offer their view, the vice president said, forcefully, "No! He won't do! His fingernails were dirty!"

That closed the discussion. There followed an awkward silence in which the various deans fought to control their urge to check their fingernails. For a moment I was taken back to my long-ago kindergarten experience, in which we children were lined up to have our hands inspected, palms up, then nails up, to make sure all was clean. Apparently the vice president had been strongly impressed by a similar experience in his childhood.

Past Positions: Line Versus Staff

Another error often made by selection committees occurs in their assessment of a candidate's past administrative experience. Committees often fail to distinguish between what I would call "line" positions and "staff" positions. A line position is one that bears direct responsibility for decisions at that level of administration. This would include department chairs, directors, deans, vice presidents/provosts, chancellors and presidents. Within the unit they head, the buck stops with them. These people have direct responsibility for policies, staff, faculty, budgets, and so on. An "assistant" or "associate" may have very limited and often highly specialized responsibilities. As an assistant dean, for example, I spent most of my time working with students. It was an important responsibility which I enjoyed, but it gave me no experience with the college's budgets, faculty problems, relations with the other colleges, or a whole host of other concerns with which the dean had to deal.

I recall looking at the curriculum vitae of a newly appointed university president and noting, with some misgivings, that almost all of his administrative experience had been in staff rather than line positions. His only line experience had been for less than one year as an executive vice president. That may not be long enough for the consequences of poor administrative judgment to come home to roost. Sure enough, the new president launched into a series of bad decisions that usually resulted from a failure to consult the people who could have given him useful information. A student could present a grievance and get the president to grant a requested remedy without his consulting the faculty member or administrator who was alleged to have caused the grievance. At the very least, such consultation might have made the president more aware that the story an aggrieved student tells may not be complete or entirely accurate, and that the faculty member involved may have a different, more complete, and possibly more accurate, version. The president's actions showed a lack of confidence or consideration for the involved faculty or administrators, and undercut them in their further relationships with students.

As another example, a donor could give something to the university without the president determining, before acceptance, the considerable cost such acceptance would require of the university. And so on. That president did not remain in office for a full year. I can't help but wonder if greater line experience at lower levels might have made him more aware of the pitfalls of making snap decisions with incomplete information.

In my experience, the strongest candidates for upper-level administrative positions are those who have successfully held some line administrative positions for a significant amount of time. That qualifier, "a significant amount of time," is important. There is in academe a

breed of administrative gypsy who jumps from job to job, and usually from institution to institution, every two or three years. As I have already suggested, sometimes the consequences of poor administrative decisions take a while to become evident. The administrator who frequently changes jobs may be staying just a jump ahead of negative consequences of bad administration. In terms of the fictional Old West, getting out of town before sunset may be a good way for a sheriff to stay alive, but does not give much indication of effectiveness as a sheriff. Selection committees should beware of such a pattern.

Perhaps the experience that best recommends a candidate is a successful run of a few years as chair of a large department. Typically such a department chair has some experience with almost all aspects of university administration. She or he will have to manage budgets, handle such faculty and staff personnel matters as salaries, tenure, and promotion, deal with students and their parents, oversee matters of curriculum and academic standards, work with researchers and their grant funds, keep track of physical plant and supply needs of the department, maintain faculty morale, assure teaching standards, and often serve as liaison between faculty and upper administration. Anyone who has successfully chaired a large department for a significant time is likely to be a good candidate for any other administrative position.

All of this leads me to:

BRYANT'S THIRD LAW OF ACADEMIC ADMINISTRATION

In searching for an administrator, what you find depends a great deal on what you are looking for, how you look for it, and who is doing the looking.

Being Recruited

The other side of the recruitment coin, of course, is being the candidate considered for an administrative position. If you have applied or been nominated for an academic position at another institution and have been invited for an interview on campus, how should you proceed?

Much of the advice one might give would be standard for an applicant for almost any position. First, take the interview seriously. The invitation represents an expenditure of time and effort in reviewing your qualifications and in hosting you for the interview, not to mention the cost of your trip to the campus and expenses while you are there. Have the courtesy to take the visit seriously. If you do not regard the job as worth serious consideration, withdraw your name as early as possible. Give yourself time to have a good interview. Do not sandwich it into a tight schedule of other commitments. Be rested and collected when you go.

Before the interview, learn all you can about the institution, something you should have done before allowing your name in candidacy. Read the catalog. Talk to colleagues who might be acquainted with that campus. If you know someone on that campus, call the person.

When you read the catalog, be aware that colleges and universities do not always live up to the pieties articulated in those documents. Still, catalogs can give you useful information and perhaps suggest questions to ask in your interview. There are the obvious topics, such as the range of subject matter offered by the unit with which you would be working and the approximate size of the institution. Then there are less direct indicators, if you take the time to look for them. For example, many catalogs list the faculty and their degrees, and perhaps the institutions from which those degrees were received. If a high proportion of the faculty in your unit lack the appropriate terminal degree in their field, you may have some questions about the quality of that faculty. Similar questions might arise based on the quality of the institutions from which the highest degrees were received. Again, if most of the faculty in your unit received their highest degree from the same institution, you may encounter cliquishness and a bland uniformity of thinking, even if that institution is among the finest. Intellectual inbreeding can be as deleterious as genetic inbreeding.

While you are on campus, be alert. What is your impression of the people with whom you will be working? What do you think of the person to whom you will report? And the people on up the line? What is the campus culture like? What is the faculty's attitude toward the programs for which you would be responsible? What are the students like? Are there problems which you would be expected to solve immediately? Why is the position vacant?

On one occasion I went to a campus for an interview for a deanship. The faculty seemed congenial, as were the other deans and directors. The vice president to whom I would have reported, who was just then assuming the position, was especially encouraging. We seemed to have very similar views about where the college should be going and how it should fit into the larger picture. I felt I could work very comfortably with this man.

My only hesitation came from my impression of the president. I could not identify any specific problem I might have with him, but I felt that he and I did not have the same approach to higher education. It was a dilemma. I very much liked the administrator to whom I would report, but I was uneasy with the administrator to whom he would report.

I was offered the position, but because of my uneasiness I decided to decline. The new vice president, with whom I felt such harmony, left his position and the institution within a year. I very well may have escaped being caught in a difficult situation. Sometimes intangible impressions are important.

On another occasion, I accepted a position, moved to the campus, and then discovered that there was very significant faculty opposition to the programs for which I was responsible. I had gotten no hint of that opposition during the interview. In fact, one of the most outspoken critics of my programs was a member of the selection committee who had been quite cordial during the interview. I might have accepted the position even if I had known earlier about the faculty opposition, but my initial activities in the new job would have been different. I am still not sure what hints I failed to pick up in the interview, but I am certain they were there. Perhaps I did not ask the right questions.

In addition to considering the institution, its people, and programs, a candidate should also take a good look at the community. First, of course, there is cost of living. A salary that might be quite comfortable in rural Minnesota or Missouri might be near poverty level in the San Francisco Bay area or New York City. As a young graduate student in the Southwest, I once accepted an editorial position in the Pacific Northwest at what I considered to be a very nice salary. When I moved my family to the new job, I very quickly discovered that costs were much higher and decent housing almost impossible to find. As a result, our quality of life decreased. I recommend that a candidate reserve an extra day during the interview visit, at the candidate's expense, to look at the community. Get copies of the local newspaper. Talk with a realtor, perhaps. Get all the community information possible and get a sense of the community atmosphere.

A candidate with a spouse would do well to visit the new campus and its community with that spouse, if the position is offered. Another set of eyes and ears can be invaluable in deciding how comfortable your family will be at the new location.

Finally, the best advice I can give is to be yourself in the interview. Be alert but relaxed. Let the interviewers see who you really are. Don't worry about creating a favorable facade. If they don't like who you really are, then you and they will not be happy together. You need to find that out before committing to a new position. Tell your interviewers what you think, how you work, and what your approach to the job would be. If you aren't going to be a good match for the people, the community, or the institution, you need to determine that as early as possible. If the people you will be working with aren't going to be comfortable with you, both you and they need to know that before any commitments are made. Remember, if you are relaxed and honest, you will give a much better interview.

3 Doing the Job: Administrative Concepts

Authority without wisdom is like a heavy axe without an edge, fitter to bruise than polish.

—Anne Bradstreet

Alpha and Omega

Beginning a new administrative job, particularly if it is a line position, is often like buying and moving into a previously owned house. When you move in, you are likely to find little (sometimes large) problems. A door does not latch properly, a rain gutter is loose or clogged, the yard is not arranged well for ease of mowing, vent fan blades tick lightly against the housing, and on and on. You find yourself wondering why on earth the previous occupant had not resolved these problems and removed such irritants that kept the place from being as comfortable as it could be.

Years later you decide to sell the house and move elsewhere. During all those years, you have solved many little, and some big, problems, redoing rooms and improving the landscaping, to the point that you have a pretty nice place to live. But when you show the house to prospective buyers, they will not be as impressed with your work as you expect them to be. That handy little shelf you put behind the sink in the laundry room, the new rain gutters and leaf guards you put up, the new flooring in the family room, the rock garden you built on that slope that was so difficult to mow, all will be taken for granted by a purchaser. When someone buys the house and moves in, he or she will immediately find little problems and inconveniences and wonder why you had never fixed them in all the years you lived there. What you did will seem to have faded into the background. What you did not get done will come to the fore.

An energetic, conscientious, creative administrator taking over the direction of a unit—department or school or college—will, like the new homeowner, find many changes that need to be made for the unit to be more effective. A few new administrators may have the good fortune to inherit a mature, well-organized, smoothly running unit that needs only to be tended carefully day by day, but those are rare in academe. I have never had the good fortune to be in that position.

So, as a new administrator, you go to work. You try to address faculty grievances that are brought to you almost before you have time to sit down at your desk. You try to find more resources, improve the unit's policies, solve (or at least ease) its space problems, revise outdated programs, initiate needed new programs, perhaps pacify disgruntled students, and in general shape up things. Through the years of your tenure you fight many battles for your unit. You gain some ground, you find good ways to do more with what you have, and you ameliorate the major discontents that can be ameliorated. By the time you are ready to leave the position, you feel that you have brought your unit a long way in the right direction. Well, sure, you know of more things that could be done, but one person can only do so much. It is difficult to fight more than one major battle at a time. And you have done a lot.

Rest assured, however, that your successor will take what you have achieved for granted, and will wonder why you did not fix the remaining problems, or perhaps foresee the new ones that are coming up. Your successor will be courteous and complementary about your achievements, all the while wondering why you didn't do a better job on that rain gutter, and why the siding on the addition is not in better condition.

The New Broom

The old saying that a new broom sweeps clean has a dangerous appeal to some new administrators. You want to wade into the mess and set things right immediately. If there is a major crisis in the unit, such drastic action may be needed. If you are already a member of the unit and know its situation thoroughly, drastic action may be effective. But beware. I have known several would-be strong administrators to come out of their corner swinging in the first round, only to discover that counterpunching and quickness are a better strategy than slugging it out, toe to toe. If there are major problems or deficiencies in a department or a college, a new administrator would be wise to explore those problems carefully and try to understand why they exist. Stupidity or laziness by your predecessor, or shortsightedness by your faculty, may not be the reason. If a new broom is not carefully wielded, it may only stir up dust and not do much housecleaning.

BRYANT'S FOURTH LAW OF ACADEMIC ADMINISTRATION

A new administrator must experience a full year's cycle of events before being completely familiar with the operations of the unit.

Administrative Styles

How should a good administrator go about doing the job? Should he or she be a leader or a facilitator?

A leader is out in front, selecting goals and directions for the unit and attempting to move the unit toward them. This means that the leader must be an idea person, with a clear concept of what the unit should be and do, and with workable plans for getting there.

Should a leader be a dictator or a persuader? A dictator must have substantial authority and the confidence of the majority of the faculty. Without these, a dictator will soon be replaced, and will probably damage the unit in the process, leaving a residue of resentment and resistance to authority. Leading does not work unless someone follows, and at a university, coercion seldom produces anything positive. A university in which coercion and intimidation are a significant administrative style will not be a very good place for either learning or teaching. One might even question whether it should be called a university.

A persuader, on the other hand, will provide the goals and the plans for achieving them, but will move only after convincing the majority of the faculty that those goals and plans are in the unit's best interests. This requires good communication and, again, the confidence of the faculty. If the majority of the faculty mistrusts a leader, even the best plans will go unsupported and will eventually fail. A persuader must be open and aboveboard in planning, must have excellent communication skills, and must be willing to incorporate suggestions and modifications from the faculty. Sometimes a leader's proposals will serve as a stimulus for faculty to come up with better ideas. A good leader will listen sympathetically to alternative, even opposing, ideas and will not become excessively defensive or stubborn in resisting them. A good leader will know when to set aside his or her own ideas if better ones come along. Good leadership focuses on results, not on ego or power.

A facilitator, in contrast to a leader, will be primarily reactive, waiting for ideas to emerge from the faculty and simply working to help faculty ideas come to fruition. When problems arise, or new opportunities present themselves, he or she will explain them to the faculty and solicit direction on how to respond. A virtue of this approach is that it is thoroughly democratic, drawing all actions from the group. A hazard is that the faculty will often be irritated by being confronted with what they will see as purely administrative problems. They will want to concentrate on their own teaching and research, leaving mundane matters to the administration. Striking a balance between consulting the faculty and tending to routine housekeeping without involving them can often be difficult.

A further hazard is that faculty members often will not take, or want to take, a broad view of the development of the department or college. They will want to focus on their own teaching, their own research, their own careers, at that particular time. They will have neither the information nor the inclination to see the wider picture or the longer term, even though those ultimately affect their personal concerns. Here again, the facilitator will have to motivate the faculty to think more broadly and to understand the implications of policies and programs for their individual careers. In such situations, the line between facilitator and leader can become hard to find.

Should a facilitator be at all proactive or simply react to the in-dicated desires of the faculty? At the least, of course, the facilitator may be faced with conflicting or overlapping ideas and have to choose which to encourage and which to assist. Sometimes a faculty member will have a good idea but not enough information to know how to implement it. In those cases, a good facilitator will help fill in details of ways and how to get the means. One great advantage of being a facilitator is that faculty who have strong objections to a proposal can be directed to its originator, a fellow faculty member. The onus of the proposal having originated with an administrator is removed, and the administrator involved can disclaim primary responsibility. He or she can claim to be "just trying to help the faculty," which of course is the one role faculty will grant as legitimate for administrators.

The ideal administrator will have all of these styles in his or her repertoire. The trick is knowing when and how to employ each. By virtue of the position, a department chair or dean will usually have more and broader information about the university than will a faculty member. This broader view may at times impose on the conscien-tious administrator a need for active leadership. On the other hand, effective communication with the faculty may stimulate good ideas that the dean or department chair can then simply facilitate. In this continuing dance of needs and ideas, sometimes it can be desirable to cause things to happen, ideas to develop, attitudes to jell, without seeming to do so. Sometimes it is necessary to be a leader in facilitator's clothing. You will not get the credit, but you will see gratifying results. On several occasions I suggested a course of action or a program, only to be met with a negative response or indifference. I continued, from time to time, to gently make the same suggestion in various forms with little result. Then, perhaps a year or two later, perhaps sooner, some member of the faculty made the same suggestion as if it were a new idea, and it was accepted and implemented. I learned to suppress the impulse to blurt, "That is what I have been proposing all along!" Instead, I judiciously observed that the idea had merit and asked the group how we should proceed. I drew smiles of recognition from a few of the more alert faculty and cooperation from most. The results are the important thing. In effect, it is sometimes desirable to be a better administrator than most of your colleagues realize. When that is the case, your own satisfaction may be your only reward.

Advocacy Roles

Outside of his or her unit, what role does the administrator play? Is a department chair or dean the unit's representative to the higher administration and wider university community—in effect, an advocate for the unit? Or is she or he the administration's representative to the unit? The effective administrator must play both roles. The administrator must function as an advocate for the unit, because he or she knows—or should know—the needs, capabilities, and goals of the unit better than anyone outside. Without a strong and persuasive advocate, the unit is likely to be starved for resources. Faculty and staff positions, expense and research budgets, and office and laboratory space are likely to drift away to other units if not guarded by a strong voice on the unit's behalf. The faculty and staff will expect the administrator to protect their interests.

On the other hand, excessive advocacy can lead to empire building, turf wars, and other forms of counterproductive unpleasantness. In times of constricting resources, it is sometimes necessary for an administrator to explain to the faculty why the higher administration has had to make some unpopular decisions. Certainly, the administrator must be reasonable in dealing with other parts of the university.

This desire to be cooperative can become a trap, however. As a new department chair, I tried to see the broader picture and cooperate for the common good. When asked to get by on fewer resources, I made strong, good-faith efforts to find ways to cut the needs of my department, exercising considerable ingenuity, I thought, in doing so. But then, the following budget year my dean said we were in a crisis again. He took the trimmed emergency budget of the past year as a baseline and asked where we could cut to meet the emergency. That became his standard pitch for every budget year as a way to free money to put wherever he pleased. The only defense was to assert firmly that there was no way the department could do its job with fewer resources, and that, in fact, more resources were desperately needed. One should be cooperative, but should not give away the family silver.

The same is true of turf wars. Departmental and college boundaries represent arbitrary subdivisions of human knowledge and should not be used to stifle teaching or research that might cross over those lines. On the other hand, if a unit's field is especially popular and active, teaching in that field really should be kept in the hands of faculty qualified by university standards to do so. Various examples come to mind. In one instance, as chair of an English department, I noticed that textbook lists for certain history courses were beginning to include novels. It was at a time when literature courses were quite popular on that campus, but history courses were not. The history department was facing declining enrollments and even the possibility of losing faculty positions.

Well, I thought, if history wants to liven up its courses with a novel or two, why not? Students who encountered novels in them might be encouraged to take a whole course on novels from our English department. The day came, however, when I found the history department's textbook lists for certain courses made up entirely of novels! That, I thought, was too much, and I sent a note to the department chair to that effect. He, a highly respected colleague and good friend, defended the practice of teaching history through novels, but the following year the number of novels in the history textbook lists dropped dramatically.

Engineering faculty often presume that they are qualified to teach almost any subject, from mathematics to history to composition to literature. They will tell you that they read a lot and are familiar with all the great writers, and therefore can teach almost any literature course. My response is that I use electricity and electronics every day. I flip light switches, use the computer, watch television, talk on the telephone regularly. I have even been known to replace a burned-out light bulb, change a broken light switch, and install a wall plug. So, by their reasoning, perhaps I should teach electrical engineering. Usually, they see my point and grant it.

Similar problems can occur in the allocation of space. I once worked for a dean who used to say that a department is like a perfect gas—it will expand to fill whatever space is available to it. Certainly an administrator should work with other units to achieve equitable use of available space, squeezing when necessary and sharing when necessary. The problem is that other administrators may not work in such a cooperative spirit. When one department is deprived of a needed seminar room so that another department can have a coffee lounge for students in a building quite near the Student Center, it may be time to raise objections, which I did successfully.

As I said, turf wars are not good things, but a responsible administrator will exercise some vigilance to keep his or her unit from being squeezed out of the picture by others less qualified but more aggressive.

One final note on acting as a unit's advocate to higher administration. When going up the line to get more resources, an administrator should give some thought to the nature of the person to whom the appeal will be presented. In short, it helps to know how to push the right buttons. I'll give a few examples of when this approach worked for me. (Listing all the times I failed would take too much space and be embarrassing. Anyway, you want to know what works. You will learn what doesn't work on your own.)

As a department chair, I worked for a time for a dean who loved to deal with crises. He considered himself very adept at crisis management and loved to have one to manage. Unfortunately, another of his characteristics was a tendency to make a snap judgment before he had all the facts and then stick to that judgment regardless of further information to the contrary. Accordingly, when I needed something from him, I learned to put it in terms of a crisis if at all possible. I would present the crisis as critical and propose that the only possible solution was one that he would find quite objectionable. When he reacted negatively to my "only possible" solution, I would grant the justice of his objection, and then say that, well, perhaps what we could do instead was what I had gone in to get in the first place. Of course, I would be hesitant about the workability of that solution, but he would override my hesitation and insist that we take that alternative solution. I would leave with what I wanted.

Another dean's favorite word was "innovation." He was sure that if we would just be innovative enough, we could get by on fewer resources than we thought we needed. I finally suggested to him that the state mental hospitals were full of innovative people, that indeed many were there because they were so innovative, but few of them should be on university faculties. As a result, we heard less from him about innovation and more about improvement, a different matter.

At another time, I worked for a university president who liked to knock people off balance at the beginning of an interview by making some extreme statement about that person's department or college. Sometimes the statements were true, or partly true, and sometimes they were pure fabrication. If you were surprised by his statement, stammered a bit, or got very defensive, the chances were poor of getting what you went to see him about. If you responded firmly, without fluster, your chances were better. If you could come back with something legitimate that knocked him off balance, you would almost certainly get what you were after. Once I learned that, I had some very productive interviews with him.

These examples sound like playing games, and to an extent, they are. However, there are some administrators with whom one should never play games. I worked with one dean who was direct, blunt-spoken (sometimes brutally so), very bright, and knew his college thoroughly. He did not suffer either fools or excuses. With him, one's best manner was to be direct, plain, and thorough. If you goofed, the best approach was to say you had goofed and explain how you would correct the error and avoid making it in the future. If your unit needed something, it was best to clearly state the specific need without exaggeration. As long as you were open and aboveboard with him, and knew your business, he was good to work for and would do all he could to help you.

Not all administrators, however, are influenced only by logic and verifiable facts. As I have already suggested, when you ask for something, it is good to consider the nature of the person whom you ask and to frame your request accordingly.

The Limits of Power

An old adage is that a university administrator has as much power as the faculty thinks he or she has. That's not true. Most administrators have considerably less power than either faculty or students think they have. The ability of an administrator to make decisions is restricted by laws, rules, policies, what the faculty will support, what the students will support, not to mention pressure from parents and alumni, and for state institutions, pressure from state officials and legislators. During the Korean War, a group of North Korean prisoners of war took over a prison camp, took hostages, and began making all sorts of demands. The U.S. Army sent a general to the camp to deal with the situation. After a fruitless meeting with the prisoners, he ordered his troops to set up machine guns around the perimeter of the camp. The prisoners took the hint and surrendered quickly. Before being sent to handle this emergency, the general had been commandant of cadets at Texas A&M University. Asked later about the dispatch with which he settled the prisoner camp problem, he said, "It was easy. The prisoners didn't have an alumni association."

An administrator's power, such as it is, comes largely from access to information. An effective administrator knows what is happening in his unit and in the university at large. Without this information, plans cannot be made, policies cannot be intelligently determined, even day-to-day business cannot be effectively conducted. When a decision has to be approved at a higher administrative level, or accepted by other units, it also helps to know something about the preferences, needs, foibles, and plans of those who must be persuaded.

On the principle that the faculty must support any decision if the decision is to survive, and the generally valid assumption that the faculty might have useful suggestions, administrative communication with the faculty is highly desirable. In the process, the administrator should share all of the information, whether or not it favors his or her viewpoint. Withholding selected details or distorting the picture will be found out sooner or later. When it is, the administrator's credibility is destroyed.

A small corollary to the principle of full disclosure is the ability, on carefully selected occasions, to show emotion. In moments of stress, certainly moments of controversy, a good administrator should remain cool, unflustered, objective, at least on the surface. Generally, such a manner will calm a situation and lead to reasoned discourse. But sometimes an administrator must show that he cares strongly about an issue. Let me give an example from my experience.

After years of neglect or simple unawareness, a strong if belated effort has developed at many universities to attract more students from disadvantaged minorities, particularly African-Americans, Hispanics, and Native Americans. I felt strongly that this effort was important and involved myself in working with minority student groups on my campus to recruit more minority students and faculty, and to provide counseling and support when they arrived. As a result, I was present at many meetings between representatives of minority student groups and the upper administration of the university. Most of the time, I was not in a position to make any of the decisions the students were seeking, so I was able to stand aside from the discussions and observe their progress.

I observed that the students brought considerable fervor to the discussion, but that the directors and vice presidents remained uniformly cool and seemingly detached. Moreover, the administrators continued to speak administratese, a language the students did not entirely understand. The result was that the students presented their ideas and grievances, and the administrators attempted to respond constructively to them, but the students heard the responses only as bureaucratic double-talk. They often left the meetings angrier than when they arrived.

It had been my good fortune to finally gain some measure of acceptance and trust from these students (as much as I could hope for as a "middle-aged white guy"). I began to examine how I had gained acceptance not given to upper administrators, some of whom sincerely shared my concerns. Two factors, I believe, were important in the difference. First, I tried to communicate with the students in plain language, not administratese. I think they usually understood my meaning. Second, I sometimes showed emotion, both in support of their views and sometimes in response to their attacks on me (early in this period, it was standard practice to "put the Mau-Mau" on any and every administrator to see what intimidation would produce). When I was attacked unreasonably, I responded warmly. I think the students then felt that I was telling them what I thought and showing them how I felt, and that I was not trying to obfuscate or dodge the issue. They were seeing a real person give an honest reaction and they accepted it as such and respected it.

On an occasion not involving minority students, showing ire and even raising my voice proved helpful. A woman on my department's faculty came to me to discuss a student who was disrupting her class to the extent that she felt physically threatened by him. I asked if she thought she could get him to come see me. She did. When the student came to my office, he was arrogant and belligerent. When I attempted to discuss the problem with him, he replied with a stream of profanity and obscenity. Getting nowhere with calm discourse, I closed the door of my office and proceeded to respond to his profanity and obscenity with my own. When he raised his voice, I raised mine. After a few minutes of this filthy shouting match, he suddenly fell silent, sat down (he had remained standing to this point), and said, quietly, "I didn't know professors knew words like that." I assured him that in my youth I had worked the wheat harvest and served in the army, and probably had learned more words than he knew. We then had a calm discussion of his problem with the class and ended with his promise to go to the counseling center for help. A couple of days later, I got a call from a counselor at the center. "What did you do to that guy?" he asked. The center had been trying to get him in there all semester, and he had finally come in. "He thinks you're the greatest thing on campus," the counselor said. "I just knew the right language," I replied, and left it at that.

I hasten to add that I have lost my temper at times when I should not have done so and made a bad situation worse instead of better. Knowing when to show emotion, and when not, requires judgment, but at the right time it can be helpful.

This all may sound calculating and insincere, but it is not intended to be so. Administration depends heavily on successful communication. When we are trying to communicate effectively, we should consider not only what we are saying, but also what the other person is hearing. Sometimes manner is as important as the specific words used. We need to constantly seek both the right language and the right manner of presentation, so that the person with whom we are trying to communicate is getting the message we are trying to convey. That's not always an easy task.

Small Survival Skills

An experienced administrator will develop a few survival techniques that are not dramatic, but may make the difference between functioning effectively and being overwhelmed by the job. I can offer three such ideas that have saved me much trouble over the years. The first is an old standard:

BRYANT'S FIFTH LAW OF ACADEMIC ADMINISTRATION

Never handle the same piece of paper twice.

This, of course, is often impossible, but the principle should remain in the administrator's consciousness. Basically, it means that once a problem or task has come to your attention (once you have read the letter or memo or taken the phone call), you should deal with it. You have spent the time reading it or hearing it. Don't put it aside and have to pick it up and read it again later. Deal with it. Do it now.

Of course, that's not always possible. Others may have to be consulted, information gathered, negotiations conducted. But the idea is sound. Do not set an issue aside because it is difficult or unpleasant, only to have it pop up repeatedly. Save time by dealing with it promptly.

The second small survival skill is:

BRYANT'S SIXTH LAW OF ACADEMIC ADMINISTRATION

Never send a letter or memo written in anger.

Sometimes you get a letter or memo, or have a meeting or a conversation that really upsets you. You sit at your desk steaming with indignation and injured righteousness. You turn to your computer and compose a letter or memo that really tells the offender off, in no uncertain terms, laying out all the points of your case with devastating logic. Good. You have organized your thoughts on the subject and let off considerable emotional steam in the process. Now put that letter in your desk drawer and forget about it for a while. In a couple of days, you may wish to take it out, reread it, and recast your argument in more moderate and conciliatory terms. Or you may just tear it up and forget it. But do not send that initial letter. That was therapy for you, but it was not effective communication about the issue.

BRYANT'S SEVENTH LAW OF ACADEMIC ADMINISTRATION

Look carefully at every piece of paper that goes out of your office over your signature.

This seems obvious, but it is sometimes easy to forget. You are desperately busy. You have other matters pressing you for attention. There is a stack of letters awaiting your signature. They are routine communications. What could be wrong with them? You fan the stack out with each signature line showing, scribble your name on each, and go on to other matters. That can lead to embarrassing mistakes.

Here are two examples of how such a mistake can occur. One was my own error, and one was made by someone else who also should have known better.

In my case, there was a large number of standard letters to prospective students. The standard text had been entered into a computer, along with a list of names and addresses to which the individual letters were to be sent. I wanted to sign each letter as an indication of at least some modicum of individual attention to the communication. The stack of letters appeared on my desk awaiting my signature. I read the top letter to assure that it was correct, and it was. The letters had all been printed in sequence in one session by one computer. If the top letter was correct, all the rest must be, also, right? In this case, wrong.

I fanned the letters out with the signature lines showing, dutifully signed each one, and sent them on their way. A few days later, an upset faculty member was in my office with one of the letters, wanting to know if I had lost my mind. He showed me a letter one of his prospective students had received. The address was correct. The opening paragraph was correct. But the middle part of the letter was gibberish. There at the bottom was my signature. Somehow, the computer had produced a number of these flawed letters, although the first two dozen or so were perfect. I need not have proofread each letter in detail, but if I had glanced at each one while signing, I would have caught the error. Because I did not, I looked—and felt—exceedingly foolish.

Another example of the need for this Seventh Law appeared more recently. I received a letter from the director of a university press concerning a publication proposal I had sent him. The garbling of several facts concerning my proposal suggested that he had not been directly involved in the matter and was writing on the basis of what he must have been told by someone else, and possibly had misunderstood. That can happen in a busy office. What especially caught my eye, and my sense of humor, came late in the letter when the director apparently tried to refer to my manuscript (which I had not sent). Instead of the word "manuscript," the letter had the word "manicurist." Where that came from I can only speculate. Perhaps a secretary had something else on her mind rather than the director's letter. In any case, a quick glance at the letter before the director signed it would have caught the problem.

Making the Rules

Academics in general have a low opinion of rules, particularly as the rules apply to themselves. Everyone else, of course, should toe the line. Some faculty, and some students, will advocate anarchy and look forward with pleasure to the chaos that would follow. But when the lights go out, or the air conditioner stops on a hot day, or there is no heat on a cold day, they will wonder why "those people" don't get their act together and do what they are supposed to do. It all depends on whose ox is being gored. Theory can construct some beautiful scenarios, but the real world (provided you assume there is one out there) may refuse to go along.

In setting up policies, procedures, and requirements (all rules by other names), most administrators prefer to be as democratic as possible, at least at the faculty level. There are always the constraints of outside accreditation, funding, and what the institution's governing board will countenance, but within those usually broad limits, the faculty should be asked to participate as democratically as possible.

In the process, one encounters a curious contradiction. On the one hand, faculty members will almost always insist that their voices should be heard in running the university. All decisions should be made democratically by the faculty. That will be the theoretical stance. In practice, however, one encounters a different story. Faculty traditionally deplore service on committees or boards. They don't have time, they say, for such red tape and bother. Leave them alone, they beg, to do their teaching and research. One encounters similar reactions from students who think there should be a student voice on every policymaking group, but who often can't find the time to go to meetings or become informed on the issues.

Democracy, if it is to be effective, is a very labor-intensive form of governance. Perhaps the university thus becomes a microcosm of the nation. If we truly want to govern ourselves, we should be willing to put in the time and effort to do so—I won't say wisely, that is too much to expect—but at least sensibly and responsibly.

Living by the Rules

Once rules are made, the administrator should play by them. Here again one encounters a curious paradox between theory and application. If, for example, a graduate council made up of elected members of the graduate faculty has established certain requirements for admission to graduate study, the graduate dean should apply those standards to applicants for admission. Usually a dean has the authority to make exceptions to such rules, but those exceptions should be rare, and they should be in cases in which the spirit of the requirement is met, but peculiar individual circumstances may not meet the letter of the requirement. The whole point of admission requirements should be to admit only those students with a reasonable likelihood of academic success. Yet even some members of the faculty body that enacted the requirements will ask that the rules be ignored. For a favorite student, or the offspring of a friend, or the spouse of a faculty member, or just a "really nice guy," the dean is asked to grant admission, even though the applicant is clearly unqualified. Such an applicant, if admitted, will likely either be coddled through to a cheap degree or will make a possibly traumatic failure. Applicants for graduate study who hold an undergraduate degree from an unaccredited college will very likely fail. Foreign students from certain regions of the world may speak English fluently, but read it with great difficulty and not be able to write it at all. The sponsoring faculty member may insist that low (or completely missing) scores on tests of English as a second language are meaningless ("I talked with him on the phone and his English is fine!"), but such a student, if admitted, is destined for failure.

So what is wrong with an occasional cheap or easy degree? Why not unbend a little and cut a weaker student some slack? What will that cost? It will cost a great deal. The majority of students at most universities earn respectable degrees, meet reasonable standards, and attain a good level of intellectual development and knowledge of their major field. When they receive their degree, the university has applied its seal of approval. With that degree, they carry the reputation of the university with them wherever they go. If the university puts its stamp on an incompetent student by giving an easy degree, this detracts from the value of every other degree it has awarded. This is unfair to all of the students who worked hard, achieved a high standard, and earned a legitimate degree. When I, as a dean, greeted new graduate students at the beginning of a school year, I told them to expect to meet high standards so that they could earn a degree that meant real achievement and of which they could be proud. We owe that to all of our good students. We also owe it to the reputation of our faculty and to the responsibilities society has given us.

As a practical footnote to this issue, I quickly learned that the information grapevine is very quick and efficient among students, particularly graduate students, and among international graduate students most of all. Very soon after I was persuaded to relax or waive a requirement for one foreign graduate student, my office would be filled with other foreign graduate students (and often members of their families) requesting similar relaxation of requirements. Their argument invariably would be, "If you waive that requirement for _____, it is only fair that you do the same for me!" I quickly learned to be very sure that any individual waiver or relaxation of requirements I might grant was based on clear, verified, and clearly special circumstances.

Some faculty seeking waivers of requirements for their pet students did not find these arguments persuasive. In that case, my response was that the requirements were not something I had established. They had been enacted by a graduate council made up of elected faculty representatives. If the complaining faculty member felt that the requirements were too stringent, or in some other way inappropriate, the matter should be taken up with a representative to the council and the council should be asked to consider it. The conversation invariably ended at that point. Most faculty want democratic process in theory, but in practice they would like the speed and efficiency of absolute authority when the action is in their favor.

This double standard may appear with faculty matters as well as with students. For example, as a department chair I assigned a freshman composition section to a senior professor. He became very angry and belligerent. What, he wanted to know, was the meaning of that assignment? I reminded him that the departmental executive committee had voted unanimously for the policy that all faculty, including senior professors, would regularly be assigned freshman composition in their turn. I also reminded him that he had been a member of that executive committee and had voted in favor of the policy. His response again illustrates the double standard. He said he had approved the policy, but he did not think it should apply to a man of his stature! Again we encounter the idea that the rules are for everybody else, but not for me. In spite of special friendships or other personal considerations, the rules have to be for everyone or you will have resentment, jealousy, and unhappiness. Your colleagues will lose confidence in your judgment and your fairness, and you will finally be unable to function effectively as an administrator, and, of course, you will constantly be asked to make exceptions.

BRYANT'S EIGHTH LAW OF ACADEMIC ADMINISTRATION

If a rule should not apply to you, it probably should not apply to anyone else.

---

4 DOING THE JOB: STAFF AND STUDENTS

*The bodily eye, the organ for apprehending material
objects, is provided by nature; the eye of the mind,
of which the object is truth, is the work of discipline
and habit.*

—John Henry Cardinal Newman

There is an old joke about the new dean bidding farewell to his predecessor. The new dean asked if the outgoing dean had any good advice to give him. The outgoing dean said yes, he had prepared two envelopes and left them in the new dean's desk drawer.

"You will see that they are numbered one and two," he said. "Do not open them until you find yourself in a real crisis for which there is no good solution. When that happens, and it will, open the number one envelope and do what it says."

"Thanks," the new dean said. "But what about the number two envelope?"

"Follow the same pattern there. Wait until your second impossible crisis, then open it and follow the instructions in it."

The new dean found the two envelopes and kept them carefully sealed until the day he found himself in an impossible dilemma for which there was no good solution. Remembering his predecessor's instructions, he opened the first envelope. Written on the single sheet of paper were the words, "Blame me."

The new dean did as he was directed, was excused for the mess he had gotten into, and went happily about the business of his college. Then, some considerable time later, he again encountered an insoluble problem and finally, hoping against hope, opened the second envelope. On the enclosed sheet were three words, "Prepare two envelopes."

Such problems are not uncommon for academic administrators, but paying attention to the people with whom one works can delay such a day of reckoning, if not cancel it altogether. Certainly, it's worth a try.

Working With Staff

A vital part of a university that is often overlooked both by faculty and administrators is the staff: the secretaries, clerks, programmers, maintenance people, and so on. The university could not function without them. A wise administrator will not only be aware of this but will let the staff people know of that awareness. If staff personnel want to work with you and help you, your life will be far more pleasant than if they don't care or are actively hostile. Let me give one example.

I once worked for an institute of technology, with one division focused entirely on applied research. That division often required the design and construction of very specialized equipment, some unlike anything ever built before. Some of this experimental equipment was very complex and had to function with great precision.

To meet the need for such special equipment, the division had its own shops, including a machine shop. The men who worked in the shops were very highly skilled. In particular, the machine shop had two expert tool and die makers. I had several opportunities to watch the engineers and scientists of the division interact with these men. There were two extremes in these interactions.

The more arrogant scientists and engineers would present the machinists with detailed plans and direct them to follow those plans meticulously and without question. On the other hand, the scientists and engineers who had a high respect for the skills of tool and die makers, and who had a personal regard for the two men running the shop, would go over the plans with them and ask for their suggestions. The difference in results from these two approaches was obvious to an outside observer.

The initial design of a complex device that has never been made before will almost certainly have flaws. A skilled machinist will often spot some or all of the flaws in the plans. Corrections made in the plans, before the actual fabrication begins, can save a lot of time and expense. However, when the arrogant scientists and engineers instructed the machinists to follow the plans as drawn, the machinists did exactly that. If they saw flaws in the design that would keep the device from functioning, they said nothing. They would simply follow instructions because no one had asked for their opinion. The result, of course, was major delays in the project and significant additional costs. In the extreme, this could be called "malicious compliance," although sometimes good-faith suggestions were simply rebuffed.

For the scientists and engineers who asked the machinists to collaborate on the design, rather than to merely obey instructions, projects ran much more smoothly. Many flaws in the designs were caught in the planning stage; others were sometimes corrected quickly during fabrication. If, after a device was constructed, it still did not work properly, the machinists took a personal interest in making corrections, doing so quickly and with considerable ingenuity.

The curious result of this situation, which seemed so apparent from the sidelines, was that the arrogant ones blamed their problems on the incompetence of the machine shop and became more imperious and demanding than before. The collaborators, however, became more and more respectful of the contribution of the machinists and consulted them ever more fully. The gulf between the two approaches simply widened.

Most of my own work with staff has been with office personnel—secretaries and clerks. These people can make all the difference in how an administrative office functions. An intelligent administrator will require efficiency and responsibility from the office staff, but in return will try very hard to keep them happy and to give them a sense of pride in the importance of their work. To the general public, to prospective students, to the parents of students, the office staff may be the first voice of the university that they hear. If the response is courteous, helpful, and well informed, both the university and the public are helped. If the response is indifferent and/or ill informed, both are harmed. Harm to the university means harm to the stability of positions at the university. This is a truth that needs to be made clear to all staff, faculty, and administrators.

I always emphasized to my office staff that they should be unfailingly responsive, courteous, and helpful to everyone who called or came to the office. Unfortunately, that standard was sometimes difficult to maintain. If a university has academic standards and honestly tries to maintain them, a departmental office, or a dean's office, will sometimes have to deliver bad news to applicants and to students: denial of admission, academic probation, academic dismissal, disciplinary actions of various kinds, necessary deadlines missed, graduation requirements not yet met. Applicants, students, and parents may be understandably unhappy when this news is delivered. In that state of mind, they sometimes want to kill the messenger. Since office staff are the first people they encounter at the university when they come to complain, they sometimes vent their anger on them. My standing instructions to all secretaries and clerks for such situations ran something like this: "We do not pay you enough to ask you to put up with such anger and rudeness. When it occurs, refer that person immediately to me. I am the official flak-catcher in this office."

Most of the secretaries and clerks in my offices were women, often but not always, younger women. In general, they were of relatively small stature. When the complainant came to the office in person, the secretary was usually seated behind a desk. For the bully in the complainant, she offered an unthreatening target for his (more often male) anger. (To be fair, when the complainants were both parents, the mother was more often the fiercer one—don't mess with her cubs.)

On the other hand, I am male, was more often somewhat older than the secretaries, stood some six feet four inches tall, weighed around two hundred pounds, and habitually stood to greet someone who came into my office. Further, as a department chair or dean, I was regarded as someone with authority. It was interesting to hear the commotion and rude, loud voice in the outer office and then observe the complainant's anger become more moderate and reasonable in my office. After a while, flak-catchers begin to notice these things. Again, to be fair, some mothers of students did not diminish their ire one bit in my office. Students usually did.

Another problem that can hinder the efficiency of an office is the fear of making a mistake. When errors of record keeping or information or communication occur, staff have a very human reaction to cover them up or blame someone else. Both reactions can create problems. An administrator who bears down hard on errors and blames and penalizes staff harshly (I have worked for such people) will have a tense organization that spends a great deal of energy avoiding responsibility. To prevent such an atmosphere, I had two standard reactions to errors in my office. First, I wanted us to analyze how the error occurred and consider how we could modify our office procedures, if necessary, to assure that such an error did not continue to occur. I was not looking to place blame on anyone. I simply wanted to know how to avoid that mistake, or that type of mistake, in the future. Did we need to clarify policy? Did the staff need to be better informed? Did we need to improve staff access to student information? Did we need new policies or restatements of existing policies? These were the kinds of questions I asked.

My second reaction was to tell the people in the office not to worry about past mistakes. If you never make a mistake, I would remind them, it means you are not doing anything. Any active, hardworking office is going to make mistakes. Our aim should be to avoid making the same mistake twice and to reduce the possibilities for mistakes by developing reasonable, straightforward procedures that will make mistakes unlikely and catch and correct them quickly when they do happen. Such an approach can create a sense of mutual responsibility and cooperation, rather than defensiveness and evasion.

A wise office administrator will soon learn to pay more attention to results than to formalities. A unit may have a beautiful organizational structure and still be ineffective. The important point is to keep focused on the results the unit is expected to produce and not worry excessively about preserving some arbitrary structure, no matter how beautiful. Keep your eye on the unit's mission, and not on the unit's bellybutton.

By the same token, pay attention to performance, not to offhand or joking remarks. When I joined a college's administrative office as an associate dean, I was assigned a secretary who made a habit of saying about her completed task that it was "close enough for government work." The first few times I heard her say this, it troubled me. Government work should be done just as carefully and well as any other kind of work, if not better, and, besides, this was university work, requiring an especially high level of quality and care. Still, I said nothing. Very soon I began to realize that this secretary's idea of "close enough" was very high quality indeed. She was the fastest, most accurate secretary I have ever worked with, and I have worked with some good ones. Her expression of "close enough" was a joke, not a statement of attitude.

In another instance, at another university, I worked in an office with a director who was extremely meticulous about formalities. He even timed the length of coffee breaks taken by the secretaries and clerks in his office, speaking sharply to them if they exceeded the allotted fifteen minutes by even two or three minutes. Quite aside from the question of whether this was a productive use of his time, while he was doing this, he was oblivious to a major morale and efficiency problem among his staff. Length of coffee breaks was the least important problem that office had, but it was the easiest to see and to measure. However, it was not the problem that was negatively affecting the productivity of the office. I finally had to point out the serious problems to the director. To his credit, he thoroughly investigated what I told him and made effective corrections.

Problems can often be avoided if the administrator consults the staff regularly and genuinely listens to what they have to say. This is particularly true when the staff member comes to the administrator with a question or with information. And it is important to show that the staff member's questions and information are taken seriously.

I once reported to a very busy director of research. I knew the director was busy, so I tried to avoid bothering him every day with questions or requests for approval of some course of action. I saved my questions and requests until I had a sizable list, then made an appointment to see the director (others just dropped in once or twice a day unscheduled). When my appointment time arrived, I went to the director's office, but often had to wait because he was always well behind schedule. I expected this and would tell my staff not to expect me back soon.

At last I would be admitted to the director's office and begin to discuss my business. Almost immediately, his secretary would tell him someone was on the telephone for him. And then another and another. My appointed time would be spent waiting for him to get off the telephone, and when the time had elapsed, there would be someone waiting in the outer office for his next appointment. This was not a calculated snub, but rather the less than organized way the director did business. It left me in the position either of delaying some activities of my unit or making decisions that the director should be making. And it left all of us (there were eight of us in the unit) feeling that our work was not high on the college's priority list. Not good for morale or for productivity. Eventually I learned to telephone him (from across the hall), with only two or three items per call. I might have to call two or three times to get through, but once he was on the line, we were not interrupted. At such times, I sometimes wondered who was sitting in his office waiting for him to get off the phone.

Finally, it is very useful for an administrator to have some familiarity with the various tasks performed by an office staff. I have worked with administrators who had not the least idea of how the tasks of the staff were accomplished. They didn't have any sense of the time—or effort—required to take dictation, or get that dictation into printed form, or enter data, or even to file documents. With the advent of computers, more administrators now have at least minimal keyboard skills, but many don't know how to work the fax machine, the copier, or other equipment in the office. Such ignorance is a real handicap. If you know how things work, where things are in the filing system, how to find your way around a database, you won't be paralyzed when your staff is not available. You'll also have a realistic sense of the time and effort that is involved in carrying out a given task. You might even be able to pitch in and help when some part of the office's function falls behind demand.

Associates and Assistants

The chair of a large department may have an associate or assistant chair, just as the dean of a college may have one or more associate or assistant deans. Usually these are fellow members of the faculty. Most often these are staff rather than line positions, with specific responsibilities within the general operation of the administrative office, although the associate title may imply that the holder will act in the place of the dean or department chair when that person is absent.

The duties expected of an assistant or associate will influence the choice of someone to fill the position. This means that the duties to be assigned should be thought out carefully before recruiting for the position. For example, when I first became a department chair, the departmental office was poorly organized, inefficient, and not very pleasant to deal with, either for faculty or for students. Accordingly, for my first assistant chair I appointed a very junior faculty member who knew how to run an efficient office operation. She accepted the position and very quickly had the office running smoothly and happily, which lifted a considerable burden from me and made students much more willing to come in with problems. She also interacted well with those students.

With those qualities, she was soon asked to run the university's advising office. She left the department, but during her time as assistant chair she made a major contribution that continued after she left. My next appointment was a more senior faculty member who assisted me more directly in the duties of a department chair. He participated in almost all of the activities of departmental administration. These two assistants were quite different in their qualifications and personalities, but each filled the role for which I appointed them quite effectively.

Having an assistant or associate chair not only lifts some of the administrative tasks of the department off of the chair, but also provides another voice in the department to explain the requirements placed on departmental administration and the reasons for various policies and decisions. The associate or assistant chair can also be a useful back channel for communication within the department, as well as an extra set of eyes and ears. These roles can also be played by an effective executive committee made up of elected faculty representatives.

In a college office, assistant deans are often asked to fill relatively narrow roles such as working with student problems, writing reports, administering fellowships and assistantships, or overseeing admissions. Associate deans may also have specific assignments, but usually these are broader and carry broader authority in the college.

Normally, there is no tenure, real or implied, for associate or assistant deans or department chairs. They serve at the pleasure of the administrator to whom they report. Still, because they are fellow faculty members and may have tenure on the faculty, removing an associate or assistant from office can be awkward. One way to avoid such awkwardness, particularly for assistant deans, is to make the appointment for a specific term—one or two years, most likely. Indeed, I have used assistant deanships as a way for junior faculty to get a taste of administrative responsibility and help them decide if they want to go into administrative work permanently. It helps them explore with minimum cost, and after their experience they are much more understanding, as faculty members, of the problems of university administration. At the same time, it helps identify those junior faculty members who will be effective administrators and those who will not. It's a good investment both ways. If the individual is effective and happy in the position, she or he can always be reappointed after the initial term is completed. If the relationship doesn't work out, either from the point of view of the administrator or of the assistant, the parting can be amicable, even graceful, when the appointment is for a specific term.

On the other hand, if an associate or assistant is not performing adequately, the dean or department chair must summon the resolve to make a change. Of all the mistakes I made as a dean, and there were many, among the worst was keeping on assistants who were obviously not doing their jobs. They made problems for students who came for help, they made extra work for the office staff, and they created problems and sometimes embarrassments for me. On occasions when I needed assistance, I had none. I let them know they were not doing their job adequately and they did move on soon to other positions, but I did not move quickly or firmly enough to minimize the damage. Do not make my error.

My father was, for much of his life, an upper midlevel civil servant with administrative responsibility for several people scattered over a wide geographic area. His administrative policy toward them was good sense and simplicity itself: "Hire people you can trust and then trust them." That is excellent advice, but you need to determine that they can be trusted and get those who fail your trust to move on as soon as possible. Going back yet another generation, my grandfather had a secretary for many years whom he came to trust implicitly. Late in her career, after years of good and faithful service, she betrayed his trust for unfathomable reasons and embezzled a large sum of money. Grandfather discovered the embezzlement, but only after an extended period. The secretary's crime cost her some years in prison. It cost my grandfather his job and broke his heart. Trust your staff, but have some unobtrusive checkpoints you can refer to from time to time. When something does not look right, don't gloss it over and hope it will go away. Find out what exactly is happening and make necessary corrections promptly.

Bryant's Ninth Law of Academic Administration (courtesy of Finley Peter Dunne's Mr. Dooley)

Trust everybody, but cut the cards.

Checking carefully does not mean that you should retain only "yes" men and women, toadies who automatically agree with everything you say. A devil's advocate can be very valuable to an administrator, protecting against the blind spots that we all have from time to time. Assistants and associates can provide valuable insights and alternative points of view and should be encouraged to do so. But when a decision is made, the assistant or associate should not only accept, but support that decision loyally. An assistant or associate who is frequently unable or unwilling to support established policies should probably resign the position or be eased out.

Working With Students

Every academic administrator, at whatever level, should keep in mind that students are the primary reason for the existence of the university. Research may be very important, but society's support is predicated upon the teaching function of the institution. For this reason, knowing what the students are experiencing, what they are thinking, what they are doing, what their attitudes are toward the university, and what their problems may be, can be essential to successful administration. How does one achieve such a level of awareness? It requires effort.

First, keep in mind the centrality of the students to the university. As undergraduates, they are not just a troublesome underclass that clutters up otherwise tidy arrangements of research laboratories. As graduate students, they are more than a cheap source of labor for the research grants.

Experience will show that students, like faculty (to be discussed later), can be extremely liberal, even radical, in dealing with other people's affairs, but quite conservative when dealing with their own. On the spur of the moment, many students can give you proposals for sweeping changes in how the university should be organized and administered, but they can be quite resistant to even slight changes in their personal lives. This was illustrated a few years ago by a news story from California. A university there set out to end, once and for all, the chronic complaints about food in the residence hall dining rooms. They hired an accomplished chef to oversee the menu and spared no expense or effort to produce the finest cuisine for their students. When they served vichyssoise for dinner and received an avalanche of complaints that the soup was cold, they abandoned the effort. Whatever the students were accustomed to at home, whether greasy fast food or cornbread, grits, and fatback, any deviation was cause for complaint. They would not adapt or expand their taste. It was, of course, impossible to meet their variety of experience.

Another hazard is the student who, for the first time in his or her life, has encountered an idea. Despite their seeming indifference to philosophical questions, most young students are latent idealists. When they encounter a formulation that neatly structures the world around them and provides pat answers to all questions, they are sometimes carried away with enthusiasm and may become zealots. These ideas might be political systems such as Marxism in one of its many forms, or a specific religious creed, or some philosophical formulation.

In the 1970s, the writings of Marcuse had such an effect on some students and contributed to a good deal of campus unrest. The only response I know is to try to show that the world is not as absolute and orderly as these students' absolutist beliefs depict it. They need to somehow learn to allow for ambiguity and tolerance of other views. And they need to learn a little humility in the sense that they might not yet, at their young age, know all there is to know about how the world works.

I encountered this problem many times, once notably in an informal discussion group of faculty and students. One of the most outspoken students was a young man who had been raised in a sheltered upper middle-class environment and only at the university had encountered ideas and people unlike himself. He held forth for a time about the utter corruption of the university and society in general. I suggested that he was too sure of the remedies for the problems he believed he saw. I said a reasonable humility was appropriate when confronting the complex problems of humanity. He made a sneering reply:

"Marcuse warned us about you Christians and your talk of humility. You think you're Jesus Christ."

"No," I responded, "I don't think I am Christ. I am just a poor disciple looking for answers. I don't pretend to know what all the answers are. I'm just trying to learn. You think you know all the answers, so perhaps you are the one who thinks he is Christ."

The young man muttered to himself but made no audible reply. Shortly thereafter he left the group. He left the university at the end of the term and got a job with a salvage company as a laborer. A year later I talked with him and found that he still had a lot to learn but had begun to expand his intellectual horizons beyond one fixed and limited ideology. He was beginning to descend from the role of Christ to being just a disciple. He had again enrolled at the university.

One good way to keep in touch with the students is to get back into the classroom on a regular basis, preferably every semester. For a busy administrator, sometimes teaching a course can be burdensome. It must be done carefully and well if it is done at all. An administrator who teaches a course grudgingly or as an afterthought will only create negative student reactions. Students pick up on dismissive attitudes very quickly and respond negatively. On the other hand, a course well taught will help the administrator to identify some of the better, more thoughtful students. When such students appear, the administrator should try to maintain contact with them even after the course is over. They can continue to supply useful insight into student life.

Another avenue is to work with student organizations, whether general service or activities organizations or specific groups such as clubs of certain majors. These can provide a general sense of student ideas and concerns, and they can supply a useful sounding board for proposals for new programs and policies. They can also help get the administrative viewpoint directly to students without resorting to the sometimes distorting medium of a campus newspaper or the rumor mill. Effective and sincere participation with student groups can also result in individual contacts with students who will feel comfortable confiding their problems and concerns privately.

Sometimes it may be desirable to help establish a new student organization, perhaps of majors in a department, perhaps campus-wide, of students at a certain level (graduate student associations, for example). An administrator must be aware, however, that such organizations can be encouraged and assisted, but they cannot be imposed. If the students have no interest, the group will fail.

A group's activity and effectiveness will vary from year to year, depending on the students involved. One should not give up on a group if it encounters a low ebb of activity for a year or two. If it is useful and can be kept alive at all, new students coming in may revitalize it the following year.

An administrator's office door should be open to students. Complaints will be more common than praise (the praise goes to individual faculty or to others), but all should be listened to carefully. One must keep in mind, however, that a given student's account of some situation may not be totally complete and accurate. Complaints, in particular, should be cross-checked carefully before any action is taken, if indeed action is needed.

On the modern university campus, most personal student problems are handled by student services people such as counselors. Occasionally, however, such problems come to academic administrators. When they do, they should be taken seriously, in conjunction, when appropriate, with the counseling service, faculty advisors, and other campus resources. Here are two examples.

When I served as an assistant dean of science and arts, my duties were primarily to work with students in that college. One morning, a young man whom I had taught the previous year in a freshman course came into my office. He had been a strong B student, attended class regularly, and did his work conscientiously. His academic background was weak, but his intelligence and hard work were overcoming that handicap, and he was succeeding as a student.

When he came into my office, he was distraught. Without pre-amble, he told me that he was withdrawing from the university. I told him that before I could sign the necessary papers, I needed to know more about the situation. He said that he had just learned that his father, who worked in a steel mill, had terminal lung cancer. The student planned to drop out of school, return home, care for his father, and help support his family. It was a plan with which I could easily sympathize, but I felt he should not make such a major life decision in his present emotional state. He needed to give the matter more thought and to look further down the road of his life. I assured him I would help with whatever administrative arrangements I could make to keep his academic career alive, once he had thought through the possibilities. I was very much afraid that if he severed his ties with the university, he would never come back. He was attending the university on an athletic scholarship in a minor sport, and that assistance might not be available if and when he returned.

The upshot was that we reduced his course load so that he could go home frequently. We secured provisional incompletes in the courses taken out of his schedule so that he could complete them later without having to pay additional tuition. He stayed in school and, after his father's death, returned to full-time study. Some years later I met him at a professional conference. He had completed his degree, gone on to graduate study and a doctorate at another university, and was currently on the faculty of a university. I wish all administrative decisions about students could have as good an outcome. Being able to help with such a problem, even peripherally (he, after all, did the work), makes the less pleasant parts of administration much easier to bear.

In another instance, inactivity seemed the best administrative path. A disgruntled graduate student wrote a letter to the academic vice president charging that a professor in his department was having an affair with a graduate student in the department. The vice president referred the charge to me, as dean of the graduate college, for investigation and recommendation. I determined that the graduate student was not an advisee of the professor, that she was not enrolled in any of his classes, and that she would not be enrolling in them for the rest of her graduate career. That removed the problem of conflict of interest or undue pressure. I recommended to the vice president that no action be taken. He was still uneasy about the situation. No determination had yet been made whether or not there actually was an affair. He wanted to investigate further. I pointed out that graduate students are generally adults. I knew this graduate student, and she certainly was old enough, smart enough, and mature enough to make her own decisions about personal relationships. The professor was in the process of obtaining a divorce and had been separated from his wife for some time. If there were no improper use of position or power granted by the university, a relationship between consenting adults was none of our business, whether the initial complaint was true or false. The vice president, who had been more accustomed to considering student problems of undergraduates, saw my point and dropped the matter. Most universities with large graduate programs have well-established policies concerning these situations, but smaller programs, particularly master's-only programs, sometimes do not. The point here is that nonaction is always an option when an administrator is confronted with a problem or complaint, but it should be a well-considered choice, not the result of inertia.

Admission of students into the university is generally handled at the undergraduate level by an undergraduate admissions office. At larger institutions, the numbers involved make the process relatively impersonal, based on grades, test scores, and other such criteria. Smaller schools may be more personal, giving weight to such factors as letters and extracurricular activities. Athletic prowess or wealthy alumni parents just might possibly have influence at times at both large and small schools. At the graduate level, many graduate college offices, in conjunction with the individual graduate departments, usually handle admissions.

In either case, the real question should be whether or not the best available indicators suggest that the applicant will succeed academically. Great care should be taken to state admission requirements as clearly as possible and to apply them as fairly and consistently as possible. Records should be kept of all decisions and how they are reached, and the process should be as transparent as possible to the applicant. This not only helps assure fairness to the applicant, but also protects the institution from lawsuits in the event of a refusal.

I recall an instance when a student with a very weak undergraduate record applied for admission to a graduate program. His low GRE scores were consistent with his poor undergraduate record. There was no indicator that suggested the probability of success if he were admitted to the program. All of his indicators were well below our published admission requirements. We denied admission. Some weeks later, I received an angry letter from the applicant informing us that he was disabled and threatening to sue us, under the Americans with Disabilities Act, for discriminating against him because of his disability. I retrieved his application record from our files and went through it carefully. Then I wrote to him and pointed out that his application contained no indication that he had a disability, so we could not have based our decision on that factor. I then explained the real basis for our decision. I told him he was welcome to apply again and that he should document his disability and outline the special considerations he felt were justified because of his condition. We did not hear from him again.

Some programs, particularly at the graduate level, prepare students for various types of professional practice such as clinical or counseling psychology, audiology, or speech pathology. Often these programs will screen students not only for initial admission, but also for completion leading to a degree and licensing. This second line of screening weeds out those students who are capable of performing adequately in the formal course work, but who are not suitable psychologically, temperamentally, or perhaps ethically, for the kind of power and authority that certification confers. This is a very difficult area, but sometimes quite necessary. It is also an area that can give occasion for lawsuits by rejected students. To assure fair treatment of students, and also to protect the faculty and university from legal difficulties, a formal evaluation procedure must be established. Such a procedure should include a thorough study of a carefully kept record of the student's progress through the program, multiple evaluations of the student, frequent consultations with the student to make him or her aware of any problems, and careful consideration of these records by a panel of qualified faculty/practitioners. If a decision is negative, there should be a clear and reasonable appeal procedure. While most of this system must be confidential, it should be kept as transparent as possible to the affected student. The procedure should always try for a balance between fairness to the student and fairness to the clients who might rely on that student's services if the student is eventually certified.

One element of fairness to the student is identifying unsuitability as early as possible in the program. To allow a student to spend two, three, or more years in a program and then declare him or her unsuitable is a terrible waste of that student's time, energy, and ambition. It is also a waste of the university's resources. There should be warning systems to detect problems early and help students to either overcome those problems or rechannel their career plans.

International students are often highly prized by academic administrators, for a number of reasons. These students contribute to the cosmopolitan atmosphere of the campus by bringing additional ranges of experience, world views, and beliefs to the campus community. They are often among the best, most highly motivated, most gifted students from their home countries. And at state institutions, they pay out-of-state tuition. Unfortunately, too many administrators want these significant positives without allowing for some of the needs of these students. The admission process for foreign students is much more complicated and requires special skills and information. Evaluating foreign transcripts can be especially challenging and require extra time and effort. When international students come to campus, they may need special support services not required by other students. In general, we must recognize that the admission of international students requires additional resources and be prepared to provide them. Otherwise, we are not meeting our responsibilities to those international students whom we admit and who come to our campus to study. They are worth the price, but there is a price to pay for their admittance.

Catching the Flak

Dealing with confrontational radical student activists can call for a whole repertoire of responses, depending upon the students' tactics. During the 1970s there was a campus joke: "The students have a list of nonnegotiable demands. The first nonnegotiable demand is that there be more meaningful dialogue." Too often, their idea of meaningful dialogue was that they talked and we listened.

On one occasion, a group of African-American students, wearing black berets, leather jackets, and aviator sunglasses, burst into the dean of students' office, shouting and slamming chairs around. The dean sat calmly at his desk until they quieted down some, then said, "Do you fellows want to take off those glasses so I can tell whether or not you're serious about this?" That calmed the situation and resulted in some useful negotiations. Afterward, one of the students involved told me about the encounter. "I don't think the dean was frightened at all," he said. I replied that the dean had been a fighter pilot in World War II, had flown many missions over France and Germany, and had once been shot down over France and hidden and later smuggled out by the French resistance. I suggested that if the Luftwaffe and the Wermacht didn't frighten him, a few students in dark glasses, black berets, and leather jackets were not likely to, either.

On another occasion, a group of Chicano students was protesting something. They kept saying "you Anglos" do this and "you Anglos" do that. Finally I said I would appreciate it if they would stop referring to me as an Anglo. I said that my ethnic background was primarily Irish and Scottish and that my ancestors had trouble with the Anglo-Saxons long before their ancestors did. Surprised, their leader stammered an explanation that he really meant non-Hispanic whites in general. I said, smiling, "I see. We all look alike to you." That raised a chuckle, and we were able to discuss the real problems in a constructive way, rather than through confrontational shouting and name-calling.

In a particularly loud confrontation with a group of the most extreme student radicals, I listened to their insults for a while and then told them that no matter how rude and insulting they became, I would not change my mind. I was still determined to agree with them. And I did. Their tactics were bad, but their grievance was legitimate, and we were able to remedy it once they stopped shouting.

Shortly after our department added a course in black literature to our offerings, a group of African-American students came to my office to protest that the course was being taught by a white faculty member. Their argument was that the black American experience could only be interpreted by someone who had lived it. They insisted that the one African-American member of our faculty should be teaching the course. I had some sympathy for their viewpoint, but explained that the one African-American on our faculty did not wish to teach the course. I had offered it to him, and he had declined. His specialty was Victorian English literature, and he preferred to stay with that. I pointed out that if we adopted the view that faculty could only teach what they themselves represented, we could only teach current literature of our own ethnic group, our own country, and perhaps of our own region. That would be a severe and unrealistic limitation for a university. No more Chaucer, Shakespeare, Donne, Milton, Austin, Thackeray, Dickens, Eliot, Sartre, Dostoevsky, and so on. And of course those writers from the Caribbean, Africa, and the Indian subcontinent who write in English might no longer be available, either. Quite a loss.

Later, the same group of students was back to ask why we did not have more minorities represented on our faculty. I agreed with them that we needed more and assured them that we were making every effort to find more, but that the supply of qualified minority faculty at that time was quite limited. Further, those who were available were being hired by larger, more prestigious universities who could pay far higher salaries and provide better libraries and other resources. The problem, I suggested, was one of getting more minority students into the universities. You can't take more out of one end of a pipeline until you are putting more into the other end of the pipeline. They still weren't convinced that more could not be done, so I solicited their help. I told them that if they, through their contacts with minority groups around the country, could identify qualified candidates, I would follow up immediately. I outlined for them what the usual requirements were for faculty positions at a university. They seemed pleased to be asked to help solve our problem.

A few weeks later, they sent to my office a list of minority candidates for me to pursue. I was hopeful when I received it. Perhaps they really could help. But then I looked at the list. It consisted of the names of minority candidates, as promised, but they were all full professors at large, first-line universities. I had to explain to the students that we were not likely to attract a tenured full professor from the University of California–Berkeley, or Columbia, or Harvard, with our assistant professorships, or even with full professorships. They finally had to acknowledge that finding qualified candidates for our positions was difficult. Involving them in the process, so that they could see the very real problems, eased their concerns about our good-faith efforts.

Graduate Assistants

Dealing with graduate assistants can be complex. A graduate assistant, whether teaching or research, is, like the administrator, somewhat of an amphibian, in this case part student and part faculty or staff. The basic rule is that graduate assistants should be adequately mentored and supervised. Perhaps no one should be allowed to teach until he or she has at least five years of teaching experience, but given that impossibility, a teaching assistant should be prepared for teaching responsibilities, and should be supervised and mentored throughout the teaching experience. To turn a graduate assistant directly into the classroom or laboratory without preparation or guidance is to exploit both the graduate student and the undergraduates in that assistant's classes. A one-day workshop before the term begins is not sufficient. The oversight must be ongoing.

It is a curious pattern that research assistants are generally prepared and monitored more closely. Can it be that research with a faculty member's name on it is considered more important than the teaching of an undergraduate class or laboratory? Surely not.

Properly prepared and mentored, almost all graduate assistants perform well, some better than some of the weaker faculty. However, when problems do develop, they should be dealt with promptly and decisively. On one occasion in my experience, a graduate teaching assistant was found to be exchanging high grades for sexual favors. He was removed immediately.

Well after midnight one night, the telephone rang at my home. The call was from a badly upset young woman who served as a graduate teaching assistant in our department. She was at the sheriff's office. She had just been arrested in a drug raid at a party on the outskirts of town. She had already called her parents and had obtained legal representation, so that was not the problem for me to address. Her call to me was for fear that she would lose her assistantship. I told her that she was innocent until proven guilty. If she were convicted of the charge, she would lose her position. Until then, she would continue as one of our assistants, if she wished to do so and was able to meet her classes. I knew her well enough to doubt that she was guilty of anything more than being in the wrong place at the wrong time. The prosecuting attorney, after investigation, reached the same conclusion and dropped all charges.

On another occasion, a teaching assistant developed a pattern of failing to meet his classes, failing to evaluate and return papers to his students, and trying to ensure against student complaints by giving everyone an A. We warned him that such behavior was unacceptable. He promised to do better, but continued in the same pattern. At the end of that term, we dismissed him from his assistantship. He then wrote an impassioned letter to the campus newspaper, alleging that we dismissed him as a sop to critics who claimed that the department in general graded too leniently. In his letter, he said that the department was just trying to "cover their ass." I wrote a letter to the paper in response to his. I said that his letter was inaccurate on one important point. We did not cover our ass. We fired him.

5 DOING THE JOB: FACULTY

Education makes us what we are.

—Helvetius

O! this learning, what a thing it is.
—Shakespeare, *The Taming of the Shrew*

A wise administrator will try to get along with everyone, but that won't always be possible. Most importantly, a wise administrator will try to get along with the faculty, or at least a majority of the faculty. That is obviously good political advice, but the best reason for doing so is more basic and essential—the faculty are the people on the frontlines carrying out the university's mission. They, and the students, are the only reasons for the administrator's position. Some (certainly not all) faculty can be cranky, irresponsible, irrational, chronically "otherwise-minded," and even outrageous, but they also are the people who do the teaching and research that justify the university's existence.

Recruiting New Faculty

In recent years, there have been relatively few openings for new faculty at most universities. Nevertheless, when an opening does occur, recruiting for it should be done with care, integrity, and sensitivity.

On one occasion, my department advertised to fill three faculty positions and received nearly 900 applications, a great many of them from people who did not have the qualifications clearly spelled out in our notice of the openings. Our first step was always to send back a postcard acknowledging receipt of the application. We did this as soon as the application arrived to save the applicant the worry of wondering if the materials had reached us. This card was obviously an impersonal standard form, but most applicants were happy to have some notice of receipt. At many institutions, an application falls into a well of silence until a selection committee, in its own time, sometimes weeks or even months later, decides what to do with it. Realizing that applications were very important to the applicant, we tried to give regular feedback and as early a decision as possible.

A great many of the applications could be eliminated very quickly, simply for lack of the specified qualifications. These applicants (who in effect had sent unsolicited applications) could be notified very quickly. We would have preferred to send personal letters to each applicant, but with more than 800 to respond to, our very limited departmental staff could not provide such individual attention. Instead, we sent each of these applicants a letter that was obviously a standard rejection letter. I tried to word it as gently and respectfully as possible, but finally a "no" has to come through as a "no." The result, sometimes, was an angry letter objecting to 1) the speed of the rejection (we must not have evaluated the application carefully, although I do not need very long to determine that a specialist in English Romantic poetry is not the person we need to teach graduate courses in linguistics or vice versa), and 2) the use of a standard letter rather than individual personal attention. The letter included an apology for the standard format but explained that the large number of applications made individualized responses impossible. For some, this disclaimer and apology was not enough. I could not find a satisfactory solution for this problem.

Once I received an angry letter from an applicant who objected in strong, even intemperate, terms to the equal opportunity statement in our position notices. That statement said, in part, that we particularly encouraged women and minorities to apply. I might have responded that the statement was required by affirmative action rules, but that would have been passing the buck. I truly did want to encourage women and minorities to apply because I felt that adding more qualified women and minorities to our faculty would strengthen it and improve the educational experience of our students. Given that belief, I would not hide behind a rule. The angry applicant was a graduate student just finishing up at a large Midwestern university. I did drop a line to his department chair suggesting that the student be counseled into a more productive approach to prospective employers. I said that I could appreciate the student's frustration in a difficult job market, but he needed to find better ways to vent his feelings.

Recruiting can have its frustrating moments for the recruiter. I once recruited a likely candidate for a deanship and persuaded the selection committee to bring him to campus for an interview. He stayed up the entire night before the interview for some family function (not an emergency) and arrived on our campus stupefied from lack of sleep. If he had sent a life-size cardboard cutout of himself for the interview, it would have been almost as responsive as he was. Was I fair in assuming he had not taken the interview seriously? He was not offered the position and I felt foolish for having recommended him.

Taking a job interview seriously might be one good indicator of the attitude one could expect from a candidate if he or she were hired and subsequently joined the faculty. I was asked by my dean to join him in interviewing a candidate for a senior faculty position in one of our social science departments. The candidate had been brought to the campus from a considerable distance (at considerable expense to the university) for the interview. He appeared at the dean's office rumpled, unkempt, wearing an old work shirt and ragged blue jeans. After the interview, the dean asked me what I thought of the candidate's appearance and dress. My response was that his dress seemed to me to be sending us a message. The candidate was saying either that he had no regard for the people who were interviewing him or that he cared little for the position and did not consider the interview of any importance. A university should not worry about a candidate dressing in high fashion (a foolish slavishness to the whims of others), but an obviously extreme effort to dress down suggests a conscious statement of attitude. That candidate was not offered a position.

Another applicant who did not take the interview seriously was a young man whom we were trying to recruit for our department's faculty. He had impeccable academic credentials, was bright and articulate, and seemed a perfect candidate for us. We brought him to campus. At the end of a day of interviews and campus and community tours, he laughingly told me that he had already accepted a position at a university in California. He had only come for our interview to get free transportation to our area so he could vacation at a nearby ski resort. In view of his commitment elsewhere, he wondered if we could dispense with the scheduled second day of our interview. I concluded that he had all the qualities we wanted except integrity.

When an applicant is offered a position, it's important to make the offer in writing and to make the letter as detailed and explicit as possible. The letter should include the basics, such as rank, tenure considerations, salary, and any other conditions, such as responsibility for teaching a heavy load of freshman introductory classes or responsibility for specific research. No matter how clear and detailed an interviewer might be in talking with a candidate about a position, we all tend to have selective hearing and selective memories. Having the conditions of employment stated as fully as possible in writing can be very helpful if problems arise after the candidate has joined the faculty. I have hired faculty for an English department who, during their interview, expressed great enthusiasm for teaching composition, only to lose that enthusiasm once hired. I have hired staff administrators in a college office who agreed readily that administrators should be in their offices during normal business hours, and especially should keep appointments made with students, only to have those staff members become very casual about their office availability to the point of missing more student appointments than they kept. Having those expectations spelled out in the letter offering the position can be very helpful at such times.

Faculty Development

Universities don't always give adequate attention to faculty development. Faculty are often given only the vaguest idea of what is expected of them and no coherent assistance in meeting those expectations. They are left on their own to develop as teachers, researchers, and participants in faculty governance and development of their academic field. The traditional culture on most campuses will make this situation difficult to change, but a thoughtful administrator will look for ways to do so.

Criteria for salary decisions, tenure, and promotion to each specific rank should be spelled out clearly. These guidelines should not be so detailed and inflexible as to straitjacket decisions, but they should establish some generally recognized and reasonable standards that go beyond criteria such as years in rank or being a nice person and a friendly colleague. Having standards gives the aspiring faculty member some sense of expectations, and gives the decision-makers (personnel committee, department chair, dean) some objective basis for decisions that will not seem so personal or biased. It is much easier to maintain a friendship with a colleague if you can tell him, "We could not promote you this year because you have not yet met the following established requirements . . . " rather than having to say, "We don't think you are good enough yet."

Untenured faculty members will often have an annual review and conference with the department chair to determine whether the individual's contract will be continued beyond the current period. For tenure-track faculty, this review should indicate the faculty member's progress toward tenure. The review should include a written summary of progress, noting in particular any weaknesses that should be addressed and remedied. This gives the faculty member an opportunity to meet the department's standards of performance. With such an annual record in the file, a tenure decision should be no surprise. The annual record should forestall any legal action by a disgruntled faculty member who is denied tenure and feels he or she was misled or not guided.

For younger faculty members, particularly those not yet tenured, various forms of mentoring may be helpful. Some schools routinely assign a senior faculty member as a mentor to each untenured faculty member. Others may assign mentors to remedy specific shortcomings. For example, I have asked particularly productive scholars to work with, and counsel, junior faculty who are having trouble publishing. Neither of these arrangements is uniformly successful, but the success rate seems high enough to justify the effort.

Another tool available to the department chair in particular is the judicious assignment of committee appointments. We want our committees to be efficient and productive, so we naturally tend to appoint the same efficient and productive faculty to all committees. This is understandable, but a thoughtful chair will try to include other faculty on a regular basis, particularly junior faculty who have not yet had committee experience. One must be careful not to cripple a committee by packing it with too many "green" members whose effectiveness may not yet be known, but a few junior people might be good to leaven the loaf and bring some fresh viewpoints to the deliberations.

Support for travel to professional meetings is another way to stimulate faculty development, as well as to make the department known beyond its own campus. Funds for the support of travel are administered in different ways from campus to campus. On some campuses, the department chair or dean may simply review all requests, approve some, and deny others. I worked on such a campus and, while I was treated very generously by this system, I don't believe that it always resulted in the wisest decisions. Personal relationships can too easily enter into the process, or at least appear that way.

Another system I have encountered, at a relatively well-funded institution, automatically provided every faculty member with funding for travel and expenses to one professional meeting each academic year. The faculty member was free to choose which meeting that might be. Since in most academic fields there is more than one professional meeting each year, the wise faculty member would ask for funding for the meeting farthest away or in the most expensive city and pay for other professional travel from personal funds. Beyond this one-meeting "entitlement," each faculty member could receive funding for any meeting at which he or she was presenting a paper or serving on a standing committee or in an elective office of the organization. This system was expensive beyond the resources of many universities, but it worked for this well-funded institution.

At another school in my experience, funding was provided for any faculty member officially involved in a professional meeting: presenting a paper, serving on a panel discussion, sitting on a committee, or holding office in the organization. When travel funding declined (while travel costs were rising), it became necessary to develop a fair way of administering less than the former level of funding. The system that was developed tried to provide reasonable support for professional travel while placing some of the financial burden for professional development on the individual faculty member. A hierarchy of support levels was established. A faculty member who presented a full-fledged paper at a professional meeting received coach airfare to and from the meeting, meeting registration charges, and housing and meals for the day on which the paper was presented (one or two night's lodging, depending on schedules). If he or she wished to remain for the additional days of the meeting, that was at personal expense. National officers of the organization received full expenses for the meeting. Panel discussants, committee members, and other less prominent meeting participants received only airfare to and from the meeting. Special participants, such as faculty asked to interview job applicants, received full expenses. This system pared travel costs to within the budget and was accepted as fair by most of the faculty. The alternative would have been to pay full expenses for a few and deny all assistance for the rest.

Human nature being what it is, there is always the question of faculty members using a paid professional trip as a junket, with no effort at professional development. Certainly I have had colleagues who spent most of their time at professional meetings sightseeing, or sitting in bars, or taking in shows or concerts, or just sleeping in. Perhaps some of these activities can be stimulating or intellectually broadening. The professor of drama certainly can benefit from attending plays in the big city, or the professor of music from attending concerts of a major orchestra. And sitting in a bar with colleagues from other schools, discussing one's field in the presence of an occasional beer, can sometimes be far more stimulating than listening to some of the formal papers presented at meetings.

Some institutions try to assure that the travel funding is used for professional development by asking the traveler to make a presentation to colleagues on his or her return from the meeting. The theory seems sound—bring back the latest ideas and discoveries and share them with your colleagues, thus increasing the benefits of the travel money. In practice, I have not seen this system to be especially productive. The presentations tend to be general and perfunctory, and the colleagues who stayed at home generally seem to have little interest.

Styles of teaching are so personal, even idiosyncratic, that systems to help faculty improve are difficult to develop and must be extremely flexible. Differences in personality and manner make what works brilliantly for one teacher a total failure for another. One device that I believe is effective, but have had only limited success in establishing, is what I call the open classroom. By this I mean an atmosphere in which colleagues routinely drop in on each other's classes. With such a practice, faculty can learn from each other, can seek and offer suggestions to each other, and can avoid the ego trip that some faculty take when they regard themselves as the absolute, unaccountable authority in their own classrooms. Under the eyes of a colleague, one tends to pontificate a good deal less and to prepare for class more carefully.

Some faculty are quite comfortable with an open classroom situation and even enjoy the opportunity. Some resist it vigorously. I worry about the teaching of some of the latter. Fear of observation always raises questions.

At one school in my experience, class observation was somewhat formalized. One classroom was set up with an "observation room" adjacent, darkened and screened so that students in the observed class could not see the observers, or even tell whether or not they were there. It was used primarily for demonstrations where graduate teaching assistants could watch master teachers, and it seemed to be very effective for that use.

I have also tried using videotape to help teachers improve, as have many others. When the cameras were permanently mounted in the classroom and could be unobtrusively operated from a more or less remote site, they had a great deal more value than when they were temporarily set up in a classroom not regularly equipped for such taping. In the latter case, their presence was too obtrusive and changed the chemistry of the class.

I once tried to use videotaping to help our master's degree candidates get teaching jobs after they completed their degrees. The job market was tight, so I thought any special feature of their application might give them an edge. I suggested that a teaching assistant could have some of his or her classes taped, and then the assistant could review them, select perhaps ten minutes out of the tapes, and we would bear the expense of making copies of that segment to be sent with job applications. The teaching assistant would make the choice of segment, could choose to send it or not, and the remaining tape would be erased and used again. I thought it was a good idea.

Perhaps I tried to accomplish too much with this idea. I asked one of our junior faculty members if he would present the idea to the graduate assistants and then work with them as a kind of overseer of the project. He said he would. I chose this particular faculty member because I thought he was capable, but for some reason he had not gotten involved in departmental matters. I thought this would give him a "service" activity and perhaps draw him into greater departmental participation. I thought it might help him get tenure, as well.

Some weeks after he accepted this assignment, he was in my office on another matter. When we had disposed of that, I asked him what progress he had made on the videotaping idea. To my considerable surprise, he exploded angrily. He said that the graduate assistants were strongly against the idea and would not participate. He said they felt it was simply a trick on my part to spy on them, and he agreed. He said he would have nothing further to do with it. I was astonished. Faculty regularly and quite openly visited graduate assistants' classes, and sometimes videotaped them, so it was not clear how these videotapes would tell us anything we did not already know, even if we proposed to review them, which we did not. I suspect this outburst was simply a cover for the fact that the faculty member had not begun the project. By that time, it was too late in the year to start, so I dropped the whole thing. I still think it was a good idea.

Meeting Special Faculty Needs

Department chairs in particular will sometimes be asked to meet special individual faculty needs. One always wants to be helpful and humane, but this area requires some care and forethought. For example, I had on my faculty a creative writer who liked to write in the morning and asked to have all of his classes in the afternoon. He was a productive writer who was publishing good work regularly. It seemed a good idea to accommodate his request, and the scheduling committee did so. Another faculty member who just did not like to get up in the morning asked for similar consideration. He did not spend his mornings working and was not a productive writer or scholar. The committee found it much more difficult to honor his request.

BRYANT'S TENTH LAW OF ACADEMIC ADMINISTRATION

It is easier to work with faculty who act like prima donnas if they sing like prima donnas.

A widely recognized professor was frequently asked to present papers at professional meetings. This required his absence from the campus, sometimes for three or four days. To offer his contribution to the broader academic world, we were happy to find colleagues to meet his classes for him when he was away from campus. In fact, he frequently reciprocated when others were ill or away from campus. On the other hand, another professor had a contract with a federal government agency, a contract he negotiated outside of university auspices. In fulfilling that contract, this professor was often absent from campus for two or more weeks at a time. He notified no one in the department of his contract or of his frequent extended absences. Instead, he personally employed a recent master's degree graduate from our department to teach his courses for him while he was gone. In effect, the university was paying a full professor's salary to have courses taught by someone whom we would have employed as a temporary instructor at best, and actually had not employed at all. In addition, this professor paid his substitute less than the portion of his salary paid for teaching those classes. He was making a profit from not teaching his courses because he was receiving a stipend from his off-campus contract. This was not fair either to the university or to the students in that professor's classes. We found it necessary to stop that practice.

Some faculty requested appointments to teach summer school as a supplement to their academic year salaries. Most of the time, these requests exceeded the number of summer appointments available. Some senior faculty felt they should have first call on these appointments, but that presented two problems. First, we were limited by the number of dollars available, so if we appointed only senior faculty, their higher salaries meant we would be able to offer fewer summer courses than were needed to meet demand. Second, in a time when faculty salaries were falling well behind inflation rates, the higher salaries of senior faculty made a summer supplement less crucial for them than for some of the lower-paid junior faculty. Our solution was to set up a regular rotation of summer appointments that guaranteed a summer appointment to every faculty member who wanted one—every other summer.

We had only one strong objection to the system. One longtime faculty member had recently purchased a house, but was overextended in the mortgage. In providing the bank with his financial statement when he applied for the loan, he had included his summer salary as part of his regular annual income. When told he would teach every other summer, he objected, on the ground that he would not be able to make his mortgage payments. In effect, he was obligating the department to bail him out, at the expense of some other faculty member. We covered him for the first summer, with the warning that we could not continue to do so. He obtained a staff administrative position that paid him for 12 months, getting us both off the hook.

New and Not so New Ideas

An enthusiastic faculty member will occasionally suggest a change for the unit—a different policy, a change in curriculum, or a new way to allocate the unit's resources. If the administrator has been in that job for a few years, and particularly if things are running smoothly and quietly, there may be a strong temptation to squelch such suggestions. In particular, some of these "new" ideas may have already been tried some years before and proven unsatisfactory. A wise administrator, however, will resist the impulse to respond negatively, or not at all. Every idea should have a fair and thoughtful hearing and its possibilities explored. Even though things might be running well at the moment, they may not continue to do so. If a unit becomes static, the rest of the university may move on and leave it behind. If the proposal was unsuccessful some years before, consider whether circumstances have now changed or whether some adjustment in the idea's application might make the difference.

One day, after I had been a department chair for some years, a young faculty member came into my office with enthusiasm about an idea for a change in the department. The department was at last running relatively smoothly and I found myself inwardly flinching (I hope it did not show) as he began to explain his idea. My inward negative reaction grew stronger as I realized that his "new" idea was one we had tried and abandoned some years before. Instead of dismissing the idea out of hand, however, I suggested he research some of its implications and promised, with that additional information in hand, to present it to the executive committee for consideration.

After the faculty member left my office, I reflected on my own negative reaction to the suggestion of a new/old idea. I concluded that it was time for someone else to chair the department. I was getting in a rut. Soon thereafter I declined another term as department chair.

The result of the faculty member's further research convinced him the time was not right for his idea, and he dropped it. He did so, however, of his own volition, not because of a negative administrative reaction.

An administrator who dismisses faculty suggestions too quickly will discourage faculty participation in the unit's progress. Change is inevitable. The trick is to find ways to constructively guide that change. I once worked for a university president who had no interest in anyone's ideas but his own. If someone tried to suggest anything contrary to his views, the suggestion was squelched bluntly and forcefully. Those who worked for him quickly learned to keep their ideas to themselves. As a result, he missed a lot of creative thinking by some able people.

BRYANT'S ELEVENTH LAW OF ACADEMIC ADMINISTRATION

Stay open to "new" ideas, even when they are old,
because the world does change.

Rule by Terror

The faculty member who protests the rules, and does so vigorously and often, may present a broader problem that must be resisted: rule by terror. When I became a department chair, my department had a small but very outspoken group of malcontents. They were generally the weaker members of the faculty—poor teachers who were unproductive as scholars and who were more hindrance than help in committee assignments. But they were accustomed to receiving special consideration in departmental affairs, because if they did not, they would cause trouble ranging from bitter wrangling in faculty meetings and complaints to the dean, to telephone calls from attorneys and threats of lawsuits. When I became chair, I felt that these malcontents should get the same consideration and meet the same standards as everyone else.

That policy elicited some storms. In faculty meetings, the group would let the malcontents talk themselves out and then quietly vote them down. Careful adherence to Robert's Rules of Order helped keep this situation under control. As for the constant threats of legal action, I learned to take several measures in response. The first was to stick to all the rules and faithfully follow all prescribed procedures in dealing with these people. Attorneys love to pounce on any deviation from established procedures, whether significant or not. The second measure was to have witnesses and to leave a paper trail. When I had a conference with one of the group, I tried to have the assistant department chair or the department secretary also present. After every such conference, I sent the malcontent a memorandum reviewing the points we had discussed and what I had said about them. Finally, when an attorney representing one or more of the malcontents called me to discuss their grievances of the moment (this happened several times), I told him that I believed the legal canon of ethics required that an attorney representing one party in a dispute must communicate with the attorney of the other party, and not directly with that party. I would then offer to provide the name and telephone number of the university's legal counsel, if the attorney did not have it. Of course, the attorney always did know the name and telephone number of the university counsel, so that ended the conversation.

The tactic of having an attorney call or write a letter to an administrator about a grievance, either by a faculty member or by a student, is common. The implication is that legal action is being considered. Unfortunately, the desired intimidation does sometimes take effect, and the administrator runs for cover, even when in the right. When an attorney makes such a call, he or she will try to engage the administrator in an extended conversation about the problem, a conversation that usually consists of questions by the attorney and, the attorney hopes, answers and explanations by the administrator. The assumption seems to be that if the attorney can keep the administrator talking long enough, sooner or later the administrator will say something that the attorney can seize upon and use as leverage. You are not being arrested, but anything you say can and will be used against you. The best response is always to refer to the university's lawyer, without further conversation or explanation. That usually ends the problem. On the very rare occasions when it has not ended the problem, questions have been directed to the university attorney, who then referred them to me. I responded to the university attorney, who then relayed my responses on to the complainant's attorney. In that way, I was protected from inadvertently giving the complainant additional ammunition.

Equal opportunity offices, by whatever name, can be valuable safeguards against racism, sexism, ageism, and other forms of discrimination on university campuses. But sometimes these offices can be manipulated, or become overzealous, in their work. There is an old saying that if all you have is a hammer, everything looks like a nail. If your job is to find unjust discrimination, you are likely to do so, whether it exists or not. In my case, it was a matter of gender and pay.

In my first two years as a department chair, our department hired an unusually large number of new faculty, almost all at the entry level. These were new assistant professors just out of graduate school. Believing that past hiring practices had resulted in too few women in tenure track positions on our faculty, I made a special effort to find qualified women to fill our new positions. As a result, the number of women on our tenured/tenure-track faculty increased substantially.

A couple of years later, one of these new faculty members came to my office and asked if the women on the faculty might get a special equity supplement to their salary for the coming year. I responded that I thought the salaries of the women were commensurate with the salaries of the men on the faculty, but if she could point out any specific instance of inequity, I would certainly do what I could to correct it. As always, of course, we were dealing with that old zero-sum bugaboo. Additional money for one salary meant less money for other salaries, so it became a matter of fairness for all concerned. If I could have conjured up additional money for the women's salaries without reducing the money for the men's salaries, I would have happily done so. No specific instance of inequity was presented to me.

I soon received a call from the campus equal opportunity office asking that I open the confidential personnel files of all of our faculty, 40-some people at that time. I was reluctant to open all files to such a fishing expedition (there were some rather sensitive police records involved, having nothing to do with the issue at hand), but I offered to provide any information they might require concerning salaries, performance, and academic experience. This was not accepted, so I suggested that the equal opportunity people meet with the department's executive committee to discuss the issue.

The two equal opportunity people who came to the meeting were both attorneys. One was older and experienced. The other was younger, relatively inexperienced, but zealous. I introduced them to the executive committee and explained the issue. I concluded by saying the attorneys wanted to look into our files to see if we were guilty of gender discrimination in the assignment of salaries. At that point the younger attorney exclaimed, "Oh, we know you are guilty. We just want to see exactly how!"

I immediately called the committee's attention to that remark and asked that they take special note of it in case there should be any question about the fairness and objectivity of the equal opportunity office's investigation. The older attorney looked pained, cut the meeting short, and the two departed. We did not hear further from that office concerning that complaint. I did supply the office with a breakdown of our faculty salaries by gender, rank, and years of experience. That data showed that, with the exception of a single individual who was providing the department with extraordinary service in a special role and at considerable personal sacrifice, the women on the faculty averaged slightly higher salaries than the men, rank by rank. There were more women in the lower ranks because of my effort to increase the number of women on the faculty, so an overall average favored the men. However, on the basis of rank and years of experience, the women were ahead. The equal opportunity office did not pursue the complaint. Soon after, in a conversation with one of the women who had made the complaint, I said I was surprised that the women felt they were discriminated against. She responded that they knew they were paid fairly. They just thought that a complaint might get them a little more money. Another form of rule by terror.

The matter didn't end there. All but one woman on the faculty dropped the matter at that point, but that one referred the complaint to the U.S. Department of Labor. This began a series of interviews with an investigator from that department. My assistant chair, who had served in army intelligence, told me right away that this man's interview techniques were derived directly from the interrogation techniques of military intelligence. I guess I was supposed to feel like a prisoner of war, but I did not. I supplied this agent with copious analyses of our faculty, each time demonstrating, I thought persuasively, that if anything, the women on our faculty were just a little better off than the men. Still he came back for more. Finally I asked him how, in the face of the information I had supplied, he could believe there was any discrimination. His response: "Until every woman on your faculty is paid as much as the highest paid man, you will be liable to charges of discrimination." At that I told him we could not meet his standard, and if he wished to pursue the complaint further, we would see him in court. We did not hear further from him or from his department. It seemed to me, throughout his time on campus, that he behaved not as an unbiased investigator, but as an advocate. He had his hammer and he was looking hard for a nail.

Sometimes a faculty member will resist negative decisions by making an appeal to the general public or to the student body. Responding to such cases requires a cool head and firm resolve. It is especially important in these cases not to be provoked into hasty action. The slightest deviation from established procedures and policies will instantly be pounced upon and used against the university. For example, in an instance to which I was simply an interested bystander, a senior professor had become manifestly irresponsible in conducting his classes. In effect, he apparently simply met with his classes and chatted randomly about whatever topic occurred to him at the time. He made no apparent effort to teach the announced subject matter of his courses. Student complaints were so frequent and numerous that the university was forced to take action. Given the professor's seniority and nearness to retirement, he was offered a research professorship which would have given him an office, full pay, and no teaching duties for the few years until his retirement. He refused on the grounds that he enjoyed meeting with students. When further negotiations failed, the university finally, and reluctantly, began procedures for dismissing a tenured faculty member.

That university, at that time, had a nationally prominent football program. When the dismissal procedures began, the errant professor called a press conference and bitterly denounced the university for overemphasis on athletics and insufficient attention to academics. Then he announced that the university was trying to fire him because of his high-minded stand in favor of academic excellence. The university wilted under the heat and discontinued its dismissal procedures. The professor returned to his irresponsible behavior in the classroom. Finally, however, the university did carry out the dismissal. Editorial writers for newspapers near all the other universities in that football conference, whose teams were being regularly defeated, had a field day denouncing this university that put football ahead of academics and fired faculty who objected. The result of the university's action, of course, was an improvement in academics.

At yet another university, an untenured faculty member was told that his contract would not be renewed at the end of the following year. In response, he began making statements to the press in favor of sexual promiscuity. This apparently was accompanied by suggestive, and often crude, behavior in the classroom. Finally he was fired on the spot to get him out of the classroom. He then made this an issue of academic freedom and succeeded in getting the university sanctioned by the American Association of University Professors. His behavior had provoked the university president into bypassing the usual procedures for his dismissal. It pays to stick to the rules, no matter how outrageous the provocation.

While serving as department chair, I became aware that a senior professor was conducting a retail business directly across the street from the campus. It was not a matter of his merely investing in a local business venture. He was actually spending much of each weekday standing behind the cash register in his store, making sales. I considered that this particular professor had retired intellectually some years earlier, so taking him away from his store was not likely to induce him to spend more time with students, or prepare for his classes, or conduct scholarly research. There were two concerns, however. One was that at least some of his students had the impression (whether true or not) that frequenting his store and buying merchandise from him would curry favor in his classes. Further, I could imagine what an investigative reporter for the local (and often hostile) newspaper might make of finding a full professor, on the faculty supposedly full-time, able to spend so much time conducting private business off campus.

I realize the rebel in some of us would say it might be good to put some public heat on the university. Those same rebels, however, are upset when the university's budget, and consequently funds for their salaries, are reduced, or not sufficiently increased, because of lack of public support.

The faculty manual contained a requirement that any full-time faculty member conducting private business must inform his or her department chair and obtain the chair's approval. The rule was developed as a way to control excessive absence from campus on consulting assignments, but it fit my needs in this case. I wrote a memo to the professor that reminded him of the rule and pointed out that he had not obtained the required approval. He was indignant and simply ignored the rule by continuing to conduct his business. I, in turn, ignored his violation of the rule. I was not going to spend my time "checking up" on how much time he spent in his store. If a reporter, or an energetic legislator, should find him spending time in his business, I could point to my memorandum directing him to desist and then take appropriate disciplinary steps. I was protected. The university was protected.

Sometimes it is necessary to protect the faculty member. A junior faculty member asked to be considered for promotion. I placed his request before the executive committee of the department and recommended that it be granted. The committee, with some justice, felt the request was premature and denied the promotion. I had the task of telling the faculty member. He was upset, and soon began efforts to find a position at another university. After a few weeks he came to my office with his letter of resignation, telling me of a position he had been offered elsewhere and which he planned to accept. As I chatted with him about it, I began to realize that he did not have a firm offer as yet. I suggested that he might want to hold off on his resignation, but he was sure he would get the position and insisted that the resignation stand.

Two or three weeks later, he came to my office in some distress. The offer at the other university had not been made firm, after all. He had resigned one position but did not have another. I simply reached in my desk drawer, pulled out his letter of resignation, and handed it back to him. I had held it on the chance that the new position would fall through.

In another instance in my own experience, I had a temporary instructor on the faculty who was hired for one year to replace a regular faculty member who was on leave for that year. During his year on our campus, the temporary instructor became the advisor for a radical student group that was very active at the time, occupying buildings and holding demonstrations. When I told the instructor (reminded him, actually) that his contract was for one year only and would not be renewed, I was accused of firing him because of his political views. When I explained to him that the position he held was needed for the faculty member returning from leave, his response was that I should just fire her and keep him. I kept her on the faculty and sent him off to rally political protest on other campuses. I did not believe that radical political views should be a guarantee of instant tenure, any more than they should be an occasion for dismissal.

During the early stages of this uproar, a tenured colleague came to my office to protest the temporary instructor's dismissal. I explained that it was not a dismissal. I was simply not able to renew what had, from the first, been a temporary, one-year appointment. The colleague said that, nevertheless, he felt strongly about the matter and handed me his resignation in protest. He then began a round of meetings with any faculty or student group that would hear him, speaking passionately about his objection and making a big issue of his resignation and devotion to principle. After a few days of this, a student came to my office to ask me if I knew the real reason this man had resigned. I said I presumed it was for the reason he gave me. The student, who worked part-time in the county sheriff's office, told me the real reason. He said that this faculty member had run afoul of the law and been caught red-handed. The sheriff, not wanting to embarrass the university, had obtained an agreement that the faculty member would leave the university and the town at the end of the school year. In return, he would not be charged. In short, he was resigning to stay out of jail, hardly the principled stand he was claiming. The humorous part of that situation was that most students knew the real reason for his departure and were laughing up their sleeves while he was proclaiming his righteous principles.

One final weapon of the academic malcontent is gossip, the rumor mill. If you can start enough negative rumors about an administrator and enough people believe any of them, you might discredit that administrator and undermine his or her support. An administrator who is constantly occupied with denying charges finally begins to look guilty, even if all the charges are false. I recall a cocktail party at which a good friend and colleague came over to me and smilingly asked if I knew that he was suing me. Surprised, I asked what he was suing me about. He said he hadn't the slightest idea. He had only just heard about it himself, on the other side of the room. Such occasions provide some justification for the old British foreign office policy of "never explain, never apologize."

On another occasion, an untenured, nontenure-track, temporary instructor became a problem for us. She made a practice of introducing herself to her students at the beginning of a term so negatively and with such stringent course requirements, that almost all of the students would immediately drop the course. The result was that a full-time instructor, with no committee or advising responsibilities, and with no expectations of research and publication, would be teaching only six to eight students each semester as her full-time load. Because the state governing board for higher education assigned faculty positions on the basis of student credit-hour production, this meant that the other faculty in the department, almost all senior to her in experience and qualifications, had to carry heavier loads to make up for her incredibly light load.

I talked with her several times about the problem. I urged her not to lower her standards but to introduce herself and her courses more positively at the beginning of each term. She steadfastly refused to make any change. If anything, she became more extreme. I hesitated to simply dismiss her because she was approaching retirement age and needed only one more year to be vested in the university's retirement system. Finally, with the agreement of my dean and the academic vice president, we arranged to move her out of the classroom and into an editorial position, for which she was well qualified. This would free a faculty position in the department and allow me to find someone who would share the department's teaching load more equitably with the rest of us.

When I presented the proposed arrangement to the problem instructor, she exploded with anger and resigned on the spot. I reminded her that she was reaching retirement age and that her retirement in the university's system would be vested in just one more year. She didn't care. She quit. I told her I would hold her letter of resignation until the end of the term, in case she reconsidered. She did not reconsider.

I talked with the academic vice president about the situation, expressing regret that her anger kept her from qualifying at least for the minimum retirement. He responded by arranging for the university to pay both her contribution and the university's contribution for one more year, even though she would not be working for the university. I thought this was a generous action and was happy that it could be arranged. Her response to this generosity was, in succeeding years, to tell anyone who would listen that I had fired her (although she had resigned and I had urged her not to do so) to keep the university from having to pay her any retirement (as if this would be of any benefit to me). This, of course, was said while she was regularly receiving her retirement checks. There were people in that community, in which I also lived, who believed her story and regarded me as a villain.

In all such problems, either with students or with faculty, the administrator is at a crucial disadvantage. The unhappy student or faculty member can say to others whatever he or she wishes about the situation, and can even go to the news media. When reporters, or others in the community, ask the administrator about the other side of the story, the administrator is bound by requirements of confidentiality, both for students and for faculty. By citing such rules and declining to comment further, the administrator may be regarded as stonewalling on an issue. In any such "trial" by public opinion, the administrator has no opportunity to present an adequate defense.

Terror tactics can be faced down, although sometimes it's a struggle. But like blackmail and extortion, if the tactics are not faced down, they will come back again and again. In the long run, it's easier to take a stand early and get it over with. I remember a professor of educational psychology telling a class I was in that children will persist in whatever behavior gets them what they want. That is also true of some who are, at least chronologically, adults.

As a sidelight to the unpleasant prospect of occasional controversy with a member of the faculty, I include a warning. Most university faculty members, particularly those in the sciences, have been educated to use the most rigorous logical analysis in their thinking. Unfortunately, they cannot be expected to apply that same level of intellectual rigor to any discussion about faculty matters involving their own interests. It has been said that university faculty are the most liberal people in the world in dealing with other people's interests, but the most conservative when concerned with their own. We might also say that university faculty can be the most intellectually rigorous people in the world in dealing with their special subject matter, but just as irrational as anyone else in dealing with their personal affairs.

One should keep in mind that university faculty are much better at analysis than they are at decisive action. Propose a plan to a group of faculty and they can find any number of possible flaws in it. That is their training and they are good at it. However, to get any decision from them, it is necessary to remind them constantly that the choice is between the status quo and the proposed plan. It is not between perfection and the proposed plan. The question has to be whether the proposed plan, whatever its possible flaws, is better than what we have now. If there are flaws, can they be corrected? To adapt the vernacular of the times, we might say that university faculty are generally better at deconstruction than they are at affirmative action.

The extremes that can be reached by this tendency to theorize without action were shown to me when I accepted a position in a university publications office. The director was a pleasant, well-spoken man who had come to our university with glowing recommendations from an old and very prestigious institution. Conversations with him about the future of his organization and what it could accomplish were fascinating. He clearly had vision. Unfortunately, he seemed completely unable to take any concrete action toward realizing his vision. Letters, reports, manuscripts, and publications would pile up in his inbox until it was almost ready to collapse. Then the pile would disappear and we would assume that he had worked very late for a few nights and cleared the box. Still, he never seemed to get anything done. Finally, he was removed from the directorship and I was asked to replace him. As I began to get familiar with the position, I checked our stock of publications. As I did so, I noticed that there were strange bundles of assorted papers on the top shelves in our storeroom. I got a ladder, climbed up, and took some of them down. They were the contents of the former director's inbox, neatly tied up with string into bundles the size of each stack that had disappeared over the previous months. Those bundles contained letters, checks, manuscripts—all the variety of materials that had come into the director's office over months, or even years. For the most part, the envelopes were unopened. It was the nearest thing to an administrative black hole that I have ever encountered in my career.

BRYANT'S TWELFTH LAW OF ACADEMIC ADMINISTRATION

University governance, whether by administrator, faculty council, or committee, has to include decisions and action, not endless theoretical analysis.

We have already observed that lowering academic standards for students devalues the degrees awarded to all students at the institution. A similar situation exists in dealing with faculty. From time to time, a department chair or dean will have to deal with a faculty member who behaves badly or who does not perform his or her duties properly. This can range in seriousness all the way from failure to meet all classes to seducing students in return for high grades, with an incredible variety of permutations and combinations in between. The administrator's first impulse may be to look the other way or to make some mild expression of disapproval. This may particularly be the case when it is not a matter of willful misbehavior, but rather simple ineffectiveness as a teacher, even if it is egregious ineffectiveness. No one likes to be unpleasant to one's colleagues.

The problem is that being "nice" to an errant or ineffective colleague may amount to being cruel and irresponsible to hundreds of students. That is hardly kindness.

Administrative Terror Tactics

If faculty terror tactics are counterproductive, so, too, are administrative terror tactics. A university faculty member who is constantly afraid of some form of administrative reprimand for the simplest action is not going to be creative or productive. Tenure can help avoid such fear, but given the other sanctions available to an administrator, the security of tenure may not be enough in the face of a strong and domineering administrator. Here's an example.

On the first day of a new semester, I went to meet my first class in a new building that had just been opened for use. Normally, I would visit the classrooms in which I was scheduled to teach some time before the beginning of a term to be sure the space was suitable for my needs, and sometimes simply to locate the room. On this occasion, I had not done so because the new building had only been open for a few days before the term began.

When I arrived at my scheduled classroom, I found a class of about 30 students gathered in a room obviously designed for seminars. It was small and contained only a large table and perhaps a dozen chairs. There was hardly space for all the students to stand in the room, much less to be seated. I told the students to stand by and I would see if the problem could be immediately remedied. They were good-natured about it and waited patiently while I went in search of a solution.

As I stepped into the corridor, I noticed that the room next door was about the right size for my class, but it only contained a professor and perhaps four students. That room was as unsuitable for that class as was the room in which my class was scheduled. A trade seemed the obvious, easy answer for both classes.

I walked in (the class had not yet begun) and explained the situation to the professor there, thinking the exchange could be made in a moment and we could both proceed with our teaching. Not so. The other class was in another college, a college with a stern, domineering dean who was very jealous of authority. The professor was polite, but he refused to make any change whatsoever without the approval of his dean. He would not even change for that one day, pending his dean's approval. He obviously felt he had no degree of freedom in managing the conduct of his own class.

Frustrated, I hurried down the hall to the professor's dean's office (the new building was for his college). The dean was not in, but the associate dean was. I explained the problem to her and she immediately agreed with my solution. However, I had to have a written note from her to convince the professor to make the trade.

Such iron discipline did not contribute to the effectiveness of that college, in my opinion.

Tradition of Mistrust

Why do faculty so often automatically mistrust administrators? Some of that mistrust may have been earned by genuinely bad behavior by some administrators. Some of it may come from believing the kind of untrue gossip I discussed earlier. It seems to be human nature to seize upon and believe the most negative stories available, particularly if they concern someone perceived to be in authority. Any observer of Internet rumors or of conspiracy theories will recognize the problem. Perhaps it goes back to the old idea that the villain is the most interesting character in most stories. In any case, it is as strong a tradition for faculty to mistrust administrators as it is for students to complain about dormitory food. No matter how good it gets, they will still complain.

Perhaps some of the mistrust comes from the healthy American tradition of skepticism of authority in general. Such skepticism is useful when it remains skepticism and does not become prejudice. With many faculty, prejudice has taken over. Allied with an all too common, and all too childish, rebellion against authority of any kind and in any form, this prejudice damages the faculty and the university. By opposing all administrators as a kind of reflex, faculty keep those who are trying to work for the best interests of the faculty and of the students from doing their job. These attitudes may keep potentially effective administrators from accepting an administrative position.

Perhaps the deepest root cause of automatic mistrust of administrators, as displayed by some rebellious faculty and by some rebellious student radicals, is their assumption that administrators are behaving as the rebels know they would behave if they were the administrators. Those who make such assumptions are, fortunately, often mistaken.

Harry Golden used to say that in any disagreement one should begin by granting one's opponent humanity. University faculty, like everyone else, should avoid stereotyping any group, including administrators. By falling into a habit of thinking in terms of "us" and "them," and assuming that "they" are in some way universally evil, faculty are not granting administrators humanity. In effect, they are behaving inhumanely, often hindering the progress of the university and their own interests.

Faculty Morale

Whatever an administrator's standing with the faculty, he or she must be concerned with faculty morale. If the faculty develop a pervasively negative attitude toward their university, or their college, or their department, or their students, or toward their responsibilities at the university, the quality of everything they do will suffer. An effective administrator will do everything reasonably possible to keep this from happening.

We have already touched upon some of the ways to maintain high faculty morale: clear and fair personnel policies, openness to new ideas, and honest concern for the conditions for teaching and research. Another way is to maintain and display a positive personal attitude toward the unit and its mission.

This last requirement, however, should not be carried to absurd lengths. Sometimes an administrator will try so hard to show enthusiasm and confidence that the entire effort becomes transparently phony and loses all credibility. Speaking at faculty meetings at the beginning of the academic year is a case in point.

A department chair or dean does not want to begin the year by telling the faculty how bad things are and how much worse they are likely to get. On the other hand, the administrator should keep enthusiasm within reasonable bounds. For example, the faculty at a small, second-tier state college need not be assured that they are part of one of the world's greatest universities. If they don't know better than that (and some college presidents seem to think that they don't), they should not be on any faculty. Faculty can recognize nonsense almost as quickly as students.

What can be done, whatever the level of excellence of the institution, is to articulate realistically the unit's mission and encourage the faculty to carry out that mission as effectively as possible. If there are challenges, they should be acknowledged, but in terms of meeting and overcoming them. An administrative Pollyanna quickly loses credibility, at least with the more discerning faculty. But an administrator who constantly proclaims defeat creates a self-fulfilling prophecy. One who presents problems as challenges to be overcome encourages the faculty to find ways to do so. I have been pleasantly surprised by the creativeness and good spirit with which faculty can sometimes solve difficult problems, given a positive outlook.

Remember the Positive

So far, I've said a lot about how to deal with problems and controversy. This is the great hazard of administration. Most faculty are hardworking, productive, highly competent members of the university community. They teach their classes faithfully and well, work hard at careful and significant research, and participate responsibly in the governance of the institution when called upon. As a result, they seldom have to deal officially with an administrator. They go about their responsibilities, and a good administrator tries to leave them alone so they can do so.

The few problem faculty are the ones who require the department chair's or dean's specific attention. It would be easy for an administrator to focus only on the problems and to think that the whole university is made up of troublemakers and incompetents. There are probably similarities in other lines of work. A law enforcement officer may feel that the world is made up of outlaws. The physician may see the world as sick. The soldier may see the world as filled with threats and conflict. Seeing the stream of problems that flows into one's office as a representation of the university as a whole is a trap that university administrators must avoid. When the losers and troublemakers dominate one's vision of the university, as they will at times dominate one's time and energy, it's time to change positions.

Preparation meant a considerable extra effort on my part (in addition to my already full load), but I wanted to give the students the learning experience they sought. The outcome could have been foretold. The students wanted the knowledge, or imagined that they did, but they were not willing to do the work necessary to gain it. Learning, for all of us, often involves hard work. For the first two or three class meetings, most of the students who signed up did come to class, but none of them had read or even looked at the material we had agreed to examine. They would not do assignments they had given themselves! In preparing for the courses, I learned quite a bit. In taking the courses, the students only learned, perhaps, that learning takes some effort on the part of the learner. For most students, particularly undergraduates, the discipline of examinations, grades, and credits seems to be necessary for steady achievement. It does, after all, give them some feedback on how they are progressing and discourages procrastination.

Some teachers in the past have graded on a curve, decreeing that a certain portion of the class gets "A"s and a certain portion gets "F"s, with the rest distributed in a bell-shaped curve between the extremes. I have no expertise in statistics, but I have been told that grading on a curve is statistically indefensible for numbers under 2,000 or 3,000 students. Other factors can affect the fairness of such an arbitrary distribution. For example, an English department to which I belonged had a fairly rigorous placement test in composition for entering students. Those who failed the entrance exam were placed in a non-credit remedial course. The rest were admitted immediately to the regular freshman composition course. Grades in the regular courses were skewed slightly to the high side because there were fewer failing grades.

Some faculty from other colleges pointed to this curve and asked if we were maintaining sufficiently high standards. I pointed out that we were siphoning off most of the potential failures into the remedial course, and that if that course did its job, those who came through it into the regular courses would be likely to pass those courses. In effect, what was being alleged a failure on our part was actually a sign of the success of both our entrance examination and of our remedial course.

The other side of that coin is the question of class grade averages skewed unaccountably to either the high or low side. In those cases, perhaps the instructor should reconsider his or her teaching effectiveness and expectations for the students. Lots of low grades might be an indication of inadequate teaching or of unreasonably high expectations. Lots of high grades might suggest low expectations by the instructor. The explanation in either case might depend on other circumstances, such as which students are in the class and what subject the course teaches.

Although high standards are certainly important, the assignment of a high percentage of failing grades should call into question the effectiveness of admission standards and teaching. I have known more than one engineering dean who addressed the entering freshman class by telling them, "Look to your left. Look to your right. If you survive the first year here, neither of those people will." It was the deans' overly dramatic way of telling the entering class that half of them would fail, drop out, or transfer out of engineering—the same as failure in the engineering faculty's eyes—by the end of the first year. Does that indicate high standards or does it suggest that there is something wrong with their school's admission procedures and/or with their teaching? Perhaps those schools are admitting students who are not qualified to do the work, or they are not successfully helping those students learn. When a student fails, it is possible that some element of the university has also failed. In any case, it's likely that the student's and the university's energy, time, and resources have been wasted in the process.

Grading and examinations sometimes raise the question of academic freedom for students, particularly in the arts, humanities, and social sciences. In these politically correct times, some faculty enforce their own particular views without allowing students their own reasoned and well-argued alternative views. In such cases, I advise students to show that they understand the faculty member's favored views. The students are not signing a profession of faith or compromising their integrity by doing so. Certainly they need to show that they understand the viewpoint presented, whether or not they personally accept it.

On the other hand, students can sometimes come up with "alternative views" that are farfetched and contrary to any kind of generally accepted reality (peace, all you amateur epistemologists). The popular Doonesbury cartoon had an episode in which a math teacher flunked a student for obvious miscalculations. The teacher said something like, "Four plus four equals eight." To which the student replied, "Not in my culture, man." There do have to be some limits.

For Faculty

Holding faculty members accountable for anything at all will prompt some cries of a lack of academic freedom. There are those who feel that once in a position on a university faculty, a professor should be given an office, a laboratory, access to the library, a nice check each month, and beyond that be left alone. I sometimes suspect that such people, when they were children, had conflicts with their parents and have still not come to terms with any form of authority or responsibility—perhaps a case of arrested adolescence. The last conversation I had with faculty who rejected any form of responsibility or accountability came just a couple of years before that particular college was abolished. I don't think our society is ready to grant that level of irresponsibility to thousands of university faculty across this land, even though a few might make excellent use of that level of freedom.

Accountability for faculty is complex. Traditionally, faculty have been expected to contribute in three areas: teaching, research, and public service. The relative weight of each of these areas varies widely. At large research universities, research accomplishment is the primary criterion for tenure, salary, and promotion, with only slight glances at teaching and no concern at all for public service. At such institutions, the research budget, including grants and contracts from government agencies, foundations, and private corporations, is usually much larger than the resident instruction budget. The heart of the administrator too often goes where the money is. At the big universities, even if the resident instruction budget is substantial, the school's reputation from research may attract enough student enrollment to sustain that budget without much attention to quality of teaching. For bright, mature, highly motivated students, the research environment with little attention to teaching can be very stimulating. They do not require teaching. They only need an opportunity to learn. For average or weak students, such a university can be baffling and even destructive.

At smaller universities and most liberal arts colleges, teaching is the primary consideration, with little or no attention to research. Indeed, I have encountered administrators at smaller schools who believe that a faculty member who publishes scholarly research must be neglecting his or her teaching duties. Curiously, these same administrators may be unconcerned or even delighted when a faculty member publishes a popular article or conducts a private business on the side. The popular article may attract favorable public attention to the school. The business on the side may provide enough income to keep the faculty member from pressing too hard for a pay increase.

Evaluation of research generally hinges on publications. The faculty member who spends years rummaging in libraries or puttering in a laboratory or studio, but who never produces anything that stands up to peer review, can hardly be evaluated as a productive researcher. Academe is rife with investigations that never produce identifiable results (not even negative results), with Great American Novels that are never completed or published, and with definitive critical analyses that never see the light of day. The trick here is to distinguish between the producer of major work that naturally requires a long time to complete and the unproductive windbag who makes a career of claiming to be on the brink of academic fame but who never produces anything.

I once worked for a dean who would literally count the titles in a faculty member's dossier. The faculty member with 20 titles was, in his eyes, superior to one with only 10 titles. He had no idea of the significance of any of the articles, the professional status of the publications in which they appeared, or even whether or not they had been refereed. His was a simple method that eliminated the need for judgment, but it was grossly unfair. Academe abounds, particularly in periods of prosperity, with tiny journals having circulations of perhaps a hundred copies and conducted by editors who network with other such editors to publish each other's work. This type of publication can hardly be equated with publication in widely circulated, widely recognized, rigorously refereed journals.

Admittedly, a dean or vice president, even a department chair, may not be qualified to evaluate specialized professional research papers in a variety of fields, nor even creative works. But some faculty within the department should be able to do so, or outside reviewers can occasionally be called upon. The use of outside reviewers is common in evaluating a faculty member for promotion to full professor. This means that someone actually has to read the work, understand it, and consider how much it contributes to knowledge in the field.

In the sciences in particular, evaluators should consider how many authors were involved and what each one contributed. Some who are mighty procurers of research grants and contracts will have money to support a whole stable of graduate students who churn out a seemingly endless string of research data which is then, like sausages, tied into links, with each link published as an article. The graduate student generates the data, sometimes with little if any oversight by the professor, but when the article is published, the professor is listed as the senior author. I have known of cases in which the name of the graduate student who did the work, and who had the idea for the research problem, does not appear even as a junior author.

Further, in many of the sciences and social sciences, almost any little packet of data can be whipped up into an article some journal will publish, whether the data are meaningful or not, and whether or not the author(s) can draw any significant conclusion from them. Indeed, if you look closely at many articles published in scholarly journals, you will see that, once you wade through the obfuscating language, the authors conclude only that they got the results they are reporting. They draw no significant conclusions other than that "more research is needed," which translates to "send us more grant money." Again, someone needs to actually read the research reports and evaluate the work's significance. Just counting titles is laziness and a failure of responsibility.

At some research-oriented institutions, research performance is measured by the number of outside sponsorship dollars attracted. I have frequently encountered scientists, and applied scientists, who, when asked how their research was going, replied not in terms of discoveries, or even of interesting investigations, but rather in dollars attracted. "How is your research going?" I ask. "Great! I got $800,000 this year," or some such sum, comes the answer, as if the purpose of the research is not to gain knowledge, but to gain money. Attracting substantial sponsorship presumably means that outside reviewers have considered the investigator's work worthwhile, so perhaps the amount of dollars attracted is an index of achievement. On the other hand, funding availability may vary widely. It can vary by field (much less for a project on ethics than for one on fuel cells, for example) and also by subject within a field. This variation may not be regulated by the judgment of significance among researchers. It is often according to priorities established by some political group in Washington. Thus dollars attracted should be used very carefully as a criterion to assure fairness across the university.

Research that is genuinely creative should be valued on its own merit and for what it contributes to other aspects of the university's mission. It assures that the faculty member is keeping current with developments in the field. Presumably, creativity and lively current knowledge will be carried into the teaching function, both with graduate students in seminars and thesis research, and with undergraduates in the classroom. Active, productive research is good insurance that a professor is not teaching from yellowed notes that are long out of date.

Evaluating creative work in the arts presents other kinds of requirements. The "popular" market is not a reliable measure alone, although it should not be discounted. Artistically trivial fiction, for example, can be hugely popular if it is lurid or sensational. The same can be true of dramas, paintings, sculpture, musical compositions, or choreography. Some sense of the quality of artistic work can be gleaned from reviews, from juried exhibits, from the caliber of publishers, from the status of performing companies or exhibiting museums, and other such indices of artistic merit. Finally, of course, there is recourse to the judgment of qualified colleagues on the same or other faculties.

BRYANT'S THIRTEENTH LAW OF ACADEMIC ADMINISTRATION

Publication is the usual basis for evaluating research and creative activity, but merely counting titles is not enough.

The leaders of most colleges and universities will insist that their primary emphasis is on quality of teaching, and in some cases it is. It is a difficult problem to adequately evaluate teaching and encourage genuine excellence in that crucial activity. I know of no foolproof way, but any system should involve both student and peer evaluation.

Student evaluation of teachers has been popular on most university campuses since the 1970s. Methods have ranged from the most simpleminded to the openly hostile to the thoughtful, complex, and sophisticated. At the lower end of this scale might be found a system inaugurated by an activist student government I once encountered. The evaluation form had a complexity that was supposed to suggest sophistication. The method of administering the form was a joke. Any student could pick up as many forms as he or she desired (Cook County's old exhortation of "vote early and often" applied here). In effect, a student could turn in as many bad or good ratings on a single professor as the student wished. A student with a grudge against a professor (even if not currently registered in the course) could turn in a number of very low ratings for that professor. On the other hand, a professor with a clique following (e.g., fraternity or sorority adviser, shared political views) could encourage his or her devoted students to stuff the ballot boxes with high praise. It was not necessary for a student to be enrolled in a course to turn in any number of evaluations of that course.

All courses were rated equally and the numerical averages for each course counted the same as the averages for any other course. Thus the average from an elective advanced or graduate course, with 5 students who chose to be there, carried the same weight in evaluation as the average from a freshman required course with 30, 50, or 300 students. One can assume that a few students who have chosen to take an advanced course in their specialty might have a more positive attitude toward the professor than a large number of students forced by curricular requirements to take a course in a subject in which, at least initially, they have no interest. That delicate nuance seems to have escaped many proponents of student evaluations.

The student-run evaluation I am recalling here had a final twist that was even more interesting. When the class ratings were averaged for each professor (we always feel so much surer when we subject the nonquantifiable to mathematical manipulation and pretend the numbers produced represent some kind of reality), all professors on the campus were lined up according to percentile score. The president of the student government, who thought up this whole system, declared to me that he would campaign to have all professors who fell below the 50th percentile fired forthwith. I suggested to him that it might be difficult to develop much of a faculty if there were a 50% turnover every year, regardless of how good the faculty became overall. He had not realized that would be the consequence. I guess he wanted the faculty to be like the children of Lake Woebegone: all above average.

Student evaluation forms that have been carefully formulated will include recognition that the same standard form may not fit all courses and all subject matter. I have dealt with student evaluation forms that included questions about laboratory exercises, something seldom encountered in classes on literature or history, for example. Nevertheless, students will go through the form and carefully fill in their evaluations, often criticizing the nonexistent laboratory sessions and giving them low ratings. I suppose the fact that they did not exist demonstrated that these laboratory classes were not much good. Or perhaps the students' rating of nonexistent elements of the course suggests the level of care and responsibility (or intelligence?) being exercised by these students as they sat in judgment of their professors. Whatever the reason for the ratings of those nonexistent laboratories, the optical scanners would dutifully note those ratings and average them into the evaluation of the course and of its professor.

More thoughtful and useful forms of student evaluation have been developed and certainly have value. They can help the instructor by providing a student's-eye view of their teaching and of the course. Sometimes an instructor will develop a distracting mannerism, will not always speak loudly or clearly enough, will digress from the subject too often, or will present other obstacles to learning. Student evaluations can point these out to an instructor who is willing to learn and improve. In this way, student evaluations, designed carefully and read thoughtfully and not defensively, can be a real help to the teacher who wants to be more effective.

Unfortunately for the lazy administrator who wants one simple indicator of teacher effectiveness, student evaluations are not reliable as the single assessment of a teacher, for a number of reasons beyond those already suggested. One of the most significant problems is what I call the hedonism factor. Most students, particularly undergraduates, when asked informally about a course or instructor, will tell you whether or not they "enjoyed" the course. They will seldom talk about how much they did or did not learn. In fact, they may not even have a clear sense of what, if anything, they did learn. A good instructor normally would like students to enjoy a course and will try to help them do so. However, teaching is not primarily entertainment, and learning sometimes requires hard work. Sometimes one has to wrench one's ideas and beliefs into new shapes as a result of learning, which can be painful. Enjoyment should be a factor of learning, not an end in itself.

To lighten up my classes, I would sometimes tell humorous stories to illustrate a point I wanted to make. Most of the time these stories seemed to be successful, prompting reactions ranging from chuckles to belly laughs. But I have found, talking with former students a year or more later, that they may remember the stories but not the point the stories were intended to illustrate. The failure was at least partially mine, but on those days I might have gotten higher ratings than I deserved. In the laughter, the students might not have been learning, but they were "enjoying" the course.

BRYANT'S FOURTEENTH LAW OF ACADEMIC ADMINISTRATION

Beware of student evaluations in which showmanship trumps intellectual content.

Current emphasis on student evaluations has, unfortunately, highlighted the hedonism factor. Put in the position of judging their teachers, students come to consider themselves consumers of education, a passive audience waiting to be entertained. There was a time when a competent teacher was one who knew a subject well and could present that knowledge clearly and coherently. The rest was up to the students. The teacher's effort to communicate was expected to be matched by the student's effort to learn. Now the teacher is more often put in the position of an entertainer who is expected to cajole students into learning, or perhaps trick them into learning while amusing them.

Given this widespread problem, administrators and faculty need to convey to students a different message about their role in higher education, a message I have tried to encapsulate in three "laws" for students. Persuading students of the validity of these laws may be a challenge, but one worth attempting.

As a teenager, I once complained to my father about a high school teacher in whose class I was having difficulty. My father suggested

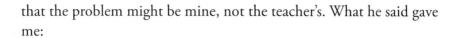

that the problem might be mine, not the teacher's. What he said gave me:

Bryant's First Law for Students

When you go to the spring for water, how much water you bring back depends a whole lot on how big a bucket you take with you.

With that, he convinced me that if a teacher knows a subject and can communicate that knowledge clearly, I as a student had a responsibility. If a student genuinely wants to learn, most teachers can teach successfully. How do we get that into student evaluations? In response to student statements to the contrary (statements some faculty have uncritically accepted), I have evolved the next two laws:

Bryant's Second Law for Students

Students are not "customers," but rather they are beneficiaries of society who owe society their best efforts to learn.

Bryant's Third Law for Students

· When evaluating a course, consider not how much you were entertained, but how much you learned.

If students can be persuaded that these "laws" have validity, both the quality of their learning and the reliability of their evaluations of teachers might improve significantly.

Student evaluations can be manipulated. As an instructor teaching freshman composition, I once tried an experiment, with the knowledge of the composition director. I had two identical sections of composition, covering exactly the same material in the same way, meeting back-to-back on the same days, with exactly the same number of students in both classes. Through the semester I had noted no clear difference in ability or performance between the two groups. Near the end of the semester, I passed out identical student evaluation forms to the two classes. As I passed out the forms to one group, I said something to the effect that my boss wanted to see how well I was teaching. As I passed out the forms to the second group, I said that these forms were intended to help me become a better teacher, and so I hoped the students would be thoughtful and candid on them.

The results were predictable. The students who were told they were evaluating me for my boss gave me very high marks, almost perfect. I interpreted that result to mean that they liked me personally, which was gratifying, and that they wanted to help me with the authority to whom I reported. It was a vote of confidence, in that they did not want me fired, but it was a slanted evaluation. The second group, who had the impression that they were speaking to me, and not to my boss, were still probably more generous than I deserved, but their ratings were not so high. I had skewed the results with just a few well-placed words.

Some evaluation systems try to defeat this kind of manipulation by having the forms administered by some other faculty member while the class's instructor is not present. This has only limited value. The instructor can set the stage in class meetings before the evaluation.

Yet another flaw in student evaluations is the inability of most students to evaluate the material being presented in the class. A professor with a good stage presence, a clear, mellow voice, and a winning personality may be presenting material that is incomplete or out of date. I recall having an organic chemistry professor who gave us material as much as 50 years out of date, long since superseded by later research. I knew it was out of date because of studies in advanced biology courses dealing with related topics, but some of my classmates took it as gospel. In literature, I have known of professors who brought fresh, well-considered, cutting-edge ideas and syntheses to their classes, and then I had one who took his lectures from old issues of *Saturday Review*. Yet the latter, who had a mellifluous voice and read his canned lectures well, was considered the better teacher. How much should count for classroom manner, and how much for intellectual content? Manner is important, but attractive presentation of poor or outdated material is not good teaching. Students generally cannot make that judgment.

Other factors weaken the validity of student evaluations. The teacher who gives everyone good grades and expects little in student performance can often get very high marks. We have already observed that the teacher of an advanced elective course with only a few students, all of whom have chosen to take the course, will likely get higher ratings than the same teacher in a large class in a lower level required course that includes students who would rather not be there.

Young instructors, very near to the age of the students, dressed most like the students, and who share the current slang of the students, often receive higher student ratings than older faculty. It pays to be cool. I recall a young teacher of poetry who read a contemporary antiwar poem to his class and concluded his presentation with the comment, "Man, that's really where it's at!" That was his total discussion of the poem and the poet. He received very high student ratings. On the other hand, a faculty member who publicly takes a political position outside the classroom, even if those views are kept scrupulously out of class presentations and discussions, may be rated lower by students who disagree.

Trivial matters, such as dress, can become a factor. I even received a long comment on an evaluation form lecturing me on what was then fashionable in neckties. It seems that the handwoven, Navajo-made neckties I was then wearing, which I rather liked, did not meet the fashion standards in effect at that time. Some time later, at another institution, the fact that I drove an ancient, battered pickup truck cast me in a very favorable light for many students. Yet these things had nothing to do with my effectiveness as a teacher.

When people are asked to assign numerical values to qualitative judgments, and then those numbers are manipulated statistically, misinterpretation becomes likely if not inevitable. For example, many student evaluation forms ask the respondent to rate the instructor on certain characteristics on a scale from, perhaps, 1 (*poor*) to 5 (*excellent*). With such ratings, an instructor's average rating on each characteristic can be determined for a class, or even for all of his or her classes. Assuming all of the specified characteristics have equal value, a single average can be calculated for each instructor by combining and averaging all of the scores. This produces a single number that can make the rating of faculty teaching very simple. I have known administrators to do exactly that. But of course there are many critical flaws in this procedure, beginning with the fact that not all of the characteristics are of equal significance, nor are students equally qualified to judge all of them. Further, this oversimplification of the process loses some of the valuable feedback that might help the instructor become more effective. For example, if all of an instructor's students rate him or her mediocre on all characteristics, and another instructor has ratings of which half are excellent and half poor, both instructors might have the same numerical average, but we are dealing with teaching situations that are obviously quite different. If an instructor gets very high marks on knowledge of the subject but very low marks on relationship with students, and another gets the opposite, they may both have the same average, but again, the teaching situation is quite different. Averages do not give us the full picture. We must look at the patterns on the individual forms to understand what the students are telling us.

For an academic administrator, another student source of evaluations comes from individual student comments. As a department chair, I tried to maintain good contact with students, particularly the majors, and I frequently got feedback from them concerning our faculty. Sometimes the report was positive, sometimes negative. When negative comments became frequent, there was reason for concern. When groups of students began coming into my office to complain, and particularly when the group included some of our brightest senior majors, as did happen on rare occasions, it was time to seek remedies. A good department chair will maintain an open office door, try to keep the confidence of students, and take their comments seriously. Still, I have found that even the most unpopular teacher will have a few staunch student defenders, and the most popular teacher will have detractors. More reliable indicators are needed.

There is no perfect system for evaluating teaching. For this reason, any system should include varied sources of information, be flexible, and as fair as possible both to the teacher and to the students who will study under that teacher's direction. As a department chair, I participated in the development of a system of teacher evaluation that I believe to be fair and reasonably reliable. Let me describe that system, recognizing that other systems might be just as good or better.

We used a brief, relatively simple form of student evaluation, with full awareness of its flaws and weaknesses. It was only one bit of evidence, and not the sole criterion for evaluation. Beyond that was a system of peer evaluation, used every year for untenured faculty, and every five years (obviously an arbitrary interval) for tenured faculty. Our reasoning was that for untenured faculty we should provide annual reviews of progress toward tenure. We tried hard to keep the number of nontenure-track instructors low. For tenured faculty, we assumed that an effective teacher one year would not suddenly become ineffective in succeeding years. This assumption, of course, saved some time and effort. We staggered the intervals for tenured faculty so that we had relatively few (obviously, a fifth of the tenured faculty) in any given year. Any tenured faculty member could also request an evaluation in off years of the cycle. This was particularly useful for a faculty member who had received a lower evaluation but felt that the evaluation was inaccurate, or that the problem that had caused the low evaluation had been corrected.

For the peer evaluation, the executive committee of the department appointed two faculty members as visitors to the teacher's classes. If the teacher, for any reason, felt that the two appointed visitors would not be fair and unbiased, or would not be competent to understand the teacher's treatment of the subject, then the teacher could select a third visitor. Each visitor was to visit a specific course at least three times consecutively. The teacher and the visitor would agree on which three class sessions, to assure that the visitor would see typical classes and not observe during an examination period. We specified that there be three consecutive visits to get a more accurate sense of how the course was presented. Even the weakest instructor may have one really good lecture in the file.

Before the visits, the teacher and the visitor would meet to discuss the aims of the course, how the teacher is presenting the material, and in general how the course is being conducted and why. After the visits, the visitor met with the teacher to discuss the visitor's impressions of what seemed especially praiseworthy and what might have been a problem. After that meeting, during which the teacher could respond to the visitor's observations, the visitor wrote a brief report covering the same points and gave copies to the teacher and the department chair. If two such peer reports seemed to generally agree, and those reports were not seriously at odds with student evaluations, the department chair could have reasonable confidence in evaluating that individual's teaching. This was usually the case, but if there were major disagreements among these sources of information, then obviously more evaluation was necessary.

Faculty and administrators in some departments reject peer review systems of this kind on the ground that it takes too much time and work. It does take some time and work, perhaps five or six hours in an individual faculty member's year. This seems a reasonable burden if we really believe our pious statements about the importance of teaching. If we want to encourage excellence in teaching, we must identify it in some reliable and fair fashion.

The third leg of the university's function is traditionally service. This term has been interpreted in many ways. I have known faculty members to offer as their service function the fact that they taught a Sunday school class or worked with a local Boy Scout troop. I do not believe that is what service means as a university function, commendable as these activities may be. There should be a distinction between what any of us might do simply as good private citizens and good neighbors, and what we as university faculty might do to serve the academic community or to make our particular expertise available to the general community. If we contribute to university governance by serving on committees and councils, if we contribute to our professional associations to advance our special fields, if we offer our special expertise to the general community then we are fulfilling the sense of university service, and should be recognized as a part of our professional accomplishment. However, the people who accept appointment to a committee but never attend its meetings, or who accept election to an office but do not carry out its duties, are simply padding their curriculum vitae. Again, making the distinction requires some inquiry and some judgment.

Finally, there is the question of tenure. Lazy administrators, when confronted with poor performance or bad behavior by a tenured faculty member, will often hide behind tenure. "What can I do? He's tenured," they wail. But they can do a great deal if they are willing to take the heat. Tenure is intended to give freedom of inquiry, freedom to espouse unpopular ideas, freedom to disagree, without reprisal. It is an essential element in a true university. We would not be the same without it. But tenure does not give the freedom to abrogate teaching and/or research responsibilities. It does not give the freedom to abuse (or seduce) students. It does not give the freedom to lie, to misrepresent, to falsify deliberately (it does give the freedom to be mistaken, a different matter). A tenured faculty member who egregiously misbehaves in some such way can certainly be discharged, although the process, quite rightly, is a complex one. But short of dismissal, there are sanctions that can be brought to bear on a tenured faculty member to encourage better, more responsible behavior. All sorts of decisions are made each year (e.g., salary increases, course assignments, assignment of laboratory space) that should be influenced by questions of accountability. If laboratory space is chronically short, as it is in most places, an unproductive researcher should not occupy prime space while doing nothing, at the expense of another researcher who pours out significant research results but is limited by crowded space. Such sanctions are available, and tenure should not be a shield against them. Tenure has become more a shield for lazy administrators than for faculty members. The result has been increasing erosion of the genuine and necessary protection of tenure.

Let me give some examples, from my own experience, of the kinds of misbehavior that fall short of requiring dismissal but should call for sanctions. In one instance, I had a steady stream of students coming to my office complaining that a tenured full professor was not teaching the announced topic of the course. Instead, he was rambling on, day after day, about the local politics of the particular political party of which he was an active member. So many students came in to complain (some of them our better majors) that I felt I had to discuss the problem with the professor. When I talked with him, he began with a charge of political bias on my part. At the time, I was a precinct committeeman for the same party, so that charge did not hold up, and he dropped it. Then he claimed academic freedom gave him the right to discuss anything he pleased in his classes. I suggested that he had an obligation to his students to teach the subject announced in the catalog for that course. That was what the students expected to learn, what they had signed up to learn, and what he therefore had an obligation to present. He had every right to express his political views, but not in that venue. Then he said he was only presenting the current political situation to illustrate the politics in the Renaissance plays he was supposed to be teaching. I told him the students were not seeing the connection and perhaps he needed to change his methods of teaching. The question of academic freedom was not put to any further test, and the professor got back to his announced topic in his teaching.

A second example was a professor who gave high grades and, of course, credits, to varsity athletes who did not attend his classes and did no work for them. This same professor was also submitting work for publication that had been previously published, without informing the editor of the second journal. When the work was published a second time, he would then list it as a new publication. When I talked with him about these problems, he claimed to see nothing wrong with such behavior and would make no commitment to discontinue it. I felt it should have a negative effect on his prospects for promotion and salary increases. A faculty grievance committee agreed.

The awarding of tenure should be done with great care, fairness, and responsibility. Every faculty member hired in a tenure-track position should have a reasonable opportunity to achieve tenure. The practice of hiring several entry-level assistant professors, ostensibly on tenure track, when only one will finally be given tenure, is reprehensible. It is deceptive and destroys any hope of collegiality among the junior faculty. In place of collegiality, it substitutes gladiatorial combat in which only one combatant is finally left standing. Such a system might have kept the Roman mobs entertained, but it does not create a true intellectual community. When a tenure-track faculty member fails to gain tenure and is dismissed, it represents a failure by the university as well as by the faculty member, and should be so regarded. As with student admission standards, the hiring policies of a university should only accept those faculty members who are capable of succeeding and are expected to do so.

A tenure-track faculty member should be given frank annual reviews of performance, conducted in a positive way to help the professor make progress toward qualifying for tenure. A weak teacher should be helped to improve in the classroom. A professor expected to produce research but not succeeding should be mentored by an accomplished researcher. Faculty development should be a much more important element than it is on most campuses.

Some institutions have a formal mentoring program for all untenured faculty. Some young faculty object to such mentoring, feeling that they can manage their own development, thank you anyway. Perhaps they can, but they should look at the matter from the administrator's viewpoint. If a young faculty member does not achieve tenure, sometimes the decision is followed by a lawsuit. The denied professor may allege inadequate guidance in meeting the requirements, or insufficient warning that he or she was not measuring up, or some other objection to the process. In such cases, it is useful to have a paper trail of written annual evaluations, written records of conferences discussing those evaluations, and written warnings about shortcomings. It also helps to have a mentoring program to show that great care was taken to provide guidance. In the best case, a mentoring program should help the young, relatively inexperienced faculty member become a better teacher and scholar. At the least, it might make an advocate of a senior faculty member who can act as a friend of the untenured faculty member when the tenure decision is made.

Colleges and universities vary widely in their expectations for teaching, particularly for research, scholarship, and creative productivity. Some will not award tenure to a candidate who has not published at least one book. Some have no research expectations but pay close attention to teaching effectiveness. Some, I'm afraid, simply go by whether or not the candidate is a pleasant, or at least not troublesome, colleague, perhaps merely requiring him or her to get along reasonably well with students. Much of my experience has been at research-oriented institutions, where research was the controlling factor in most departments.

An active researcher who does significant work and brings the expertise and enthusiasm of the committed researcher to the classroom is a great asset to a university and should be recognized and rewarded. On the other hand, the majority of the faculty of colleges and universities in this country are not dedicated and productive researchers. If they find themselves at a research-oriented university, they are driven to publish something, anything, to survive. The result, nationally, has been a burgeoning mountain of trivial, often meaningless publication. Some of it is polysyllabic drivel that clutters up the channels of academic communication and wastes the time of the author's colleagues. Much of it consists of efforts to catch the wave of the current intellectual fashion. In an effort to reduce this flood of nonsense, I have suggested to my university's administration that there be two sets of criteria for faculty performance. One would be the traditional one, requiring teaching, research, and service. As is usually the case, the teaching load would be adjusted to allow time for meaningful research. A faculty member who declares himself or herself to be a researcher would be evaluated by these criteria.

The other set of criteria would be for faculty members who declare themselves to be teachers only and not researchers. They would carry a heavier teaching load and would stand or fall by their performance as teachers. One standard of evaluation would be that their teaching stays current with developments in the field (no 50-year-old, outdated theory). These faculty could publish if and when they had something they would really like to say to the profession, but they would have no compulsion to grind out reams of windy jargon or pointless data just to survive. The result might be more good teaching and less bad publishing. I was never able to sell this idea to the upper administration, but I still believe it would be a valuable advancement in faculty evaluation.

Many faculty resist even the hint of accountability. Certainly it can be turned into restriction of academic freedom, and that should be resisted. But there must be accountability. Our society insists upon it. We should develop our own carefully considered, balanced, fair criteria for accountability. If we do not, more restrictive and dangerous systems will be imposed upon us by people who do not fully understand what a university is and how it works. Worse yet, these people may neither understand nor appreciate academic freedom.

For Administrators

Accountability for administrators may take various forms, and may involve risks as well as benefits. To the extent that the administrator serves at the pleasure of the next administrator up in the chain of responsibility, right through the president to the governing board, the key to longevity in office lies in keeping the boss happy. The value in this approach, for the university, depends on the nature of the boss. If the administrators up the line have good judgment and a real desire for excellence, then keeping the boss happy can produce positive results. If any or all of the administrators up the line are only concerned with keeping their own lives pleasant and their positions secure, this approach can produce administrators who are chiefly concerned with keeping their units quiet and trouble-free. In this mode, students or faculty who threaten to raise a fuss about anything will be placated at all costs, regardless of fairness to other students or faculty, and regardless of academic standards. "Don't rock the boat" becomes the unit motto.

A more effective mode of accountability is a regularly scheduled review of the unit and of the unit administrator's performance. The interval for these reviews is arbitrary. I have found six years to be a good interval, although it could be more or less. Too short an interval keeps the unit in a constant state of self-study and takes too much time away from the real business of the university. Too great an interval may allow administrative abuse or incompetence to go unchecked long enough to do lasting damage to the unit. For serious administrative problems, there should be some provision for a substantial majority of the faculty, or for a responsible administrator, to institute a review before the scheduled time.

The review should begin with a self-study conducted by an elected committee of the unit's faculty, plus at least one faculty member from outside the unit who is appointed by a higher-level administrator. The outside member should be responsible to the appointing administrator and should report on the balance, thoroughness, and fairness of the self-study. The committee should survey all of the unit's faculty, making each faculty evaulation anonymous, to encourage frankness and remove the threat of reprisal for negative comments. The committee should also survey the non-academic staff and a good sample of students majoring in the unit.

These surveys essentially indicate morale in the unit. Happy faculty, staff, and students suggest a well-run unit, but do not prove that it is fulfilling the purposes of a university. Other indicators of the unit's effectiveness must also be considered. The quality of the teaching in the unit may be indicated by teaching evaluations over the years, by the performance of its students on generally recognized examinations (GREs, various state professional examinations, etc.), and by the careers of graduates from the unit over the past few years. Graduates of the unit might be surveyed along with current students. I have found that former students only come to realize how much they have learned, or not learned, years after leaving school.

In evaluating the performance of graduates, one should take the value-added approach. If the institution is elite, attracting and admitting only the most talented students, then those students should be expected to achieve impressively after graduation. On the other hand, less should be expected of students who graduate from a second- or third-tier institution that admits average students, perhaps the ones rejected by the elite schools. The expectation for those students might be one of productive competence rather than world-class brilliance.

Research productivity might also be considered. Is scholarly research encouraged, stimulated, and adequately supported? Are there administrative policies or behaviors that especially help or hinder such activities?

In the area of service, how much do the unit administrator and faculty contribute to the governance of the university and to the operations of relevant professional societies? What is the unit's reputation or status with the rest of the university and within the academic world?

The evaluation needs to address these questions of productivity and status, in addition to the questions of morale, to safeguard against a situation in which the administrator is trying to motivate a smugly unproductive unit out of its lethargy and into effective performance. A good administrator will maintain high morale in the unit, but sometimes a unit settles comfortably into a rut of mediocrity and resents being urged to leave it. The evaluating administrators must use that rare commodity, good judgment, in considering the results of the study of a unit. Changing the culture of a faculty can be painful, both for the faculty and for the administrator, and should not be attempted lightly. When a change must be made, sometimes a Fabian approach is best, but even in gradual change, toes may be stepped upon and fears raised. Allowances must be made for administrators caught in this situation.

I was once in such a situation. At the outset, a substantial minority of the faculty were unhappy with my efforts to develop the program and improve its quality. They feared that my efforts would interfere with their quiet, comfortable, and undemanding academic life. They felt threatened and said so in many ways. Fortunately, the upper administration, who had hired me for just such an effort, stayed with me through the early unrest. As the program developed, many of the faculty who had been uneasy found how much more pleasant it can be to teach students who are well prepared and highly motivated and in the enviornment of a well-developed, complete curriculum.

Ultimately, the great majority of the faculty supported what we had been trying to do. Incidentally, I was also able to remove some of the burdens that they feared I would increase. Overall, I believe their reaction was positive. In essence, you can sometimes buck the tide of faculty sentiment for a short time, but you had better get visible results that the majority of the faculty will ultimately approve. Otherwise you may be headed for defeat and dismissal. There are times when it might be preferable to risk defeat and departure from the job than be a willing party to a situation that you consider unacceptable. Here Bryant's First Law comes into play: No one should have an administrative position who wants it. No administrator should quit over every little disagreement in policy, but a conscientious administrator may finally have to decide where to draw the line. At this point it becomes accountability with one's own conscience. No administrator should want the job badly enough to compromise her or his own basic principles. Administrative actions should be based on something more than pleasing the boss and keeping one's job.

1 THE BUDGET AND RESOURCES MAZE

Knowledge itself is power.

—Francis Bacon

Most academics who fumble their way into administrative positions would rather deal with courses, curricula, attracting good students and faculty, and other such interesting policy questions. Many prefer not to deal with such crass details as money, classroom space, or laboratory equipment. But sooner or later, these questions must be addressed. A good administrator must learn to read the university's budget and space-allocation reports. Every university has its own accounting methods and its own format for computer printouts. A responsible administrator must learn to read and understand them. If the format is not clear, he or she should communicate with the accounting office until everything is clearly explained. I have found that insisting upon full and clear explanations can turn up startling inequities in accounting methods. In fact, on occasion I believe that accountants have deliberately obfuscated to conceal inequities that they know exist and wish to preserve because they make the accountant's task simpler. I suspect that some university accountants believe that the purpose of the university is to provide something for them to keep books on. The university, they assume, should serve them, and not the other way around.

As an extension of this problem, there were several times in the accounting office and in the registrar's office when I was told that a desirable change in university policy, approved by the faculty, could not be implemented because a computer program did not allow for it. In effect, I was being told that the university should conform to a given computer program, rather than the computer program meeting the needs of the university. There is always the hazard of such attitudes allowing the tail to wag the dog.

Once the reading of financial printouts has been mastered, it is necessary to check them for the unit every month. The most astonishing things can appear on those budgets if they are not watched carefully: charges against the department or college of which the unit knows nothing, failures to credit the department or college with money brought to the financial office, and so on. It is perhaps not coincidental that once the administrator begins monitoring the monthly statements carefully and refuses to accept obscure double-talk in explanation, the errors in that unit's accounts are reduced significantly.

Keeping track of funds that your unit directly receives, without first passing through the university's accounting office, must also be done very carefully. When funds come in directly, some administrators may be tempted to regard them as purely discretionary. That is a trap the responsible administrator will not fall into. Sooner or later there will be an audit. A careful, accurate, complete paper trail that can justify the handling of all such funds must be maintained.

When I became responsible for one graduate school's budget, there was an application fee for admission to graduate study. The fee was presumably to help cover the cost of processing the application. To my surprise, however, I found that the money collected did not stay in the graduate school's budget. It went into the university's general fund, and it soon became evident that increasing the number of applications did not increase the budget or staff of the graduate school. In a further complication, when the graduate school turned the application fees over to the university financial office, no receipt was given (although requested), and all record of that money disappeared. In the case of some thousands of dollars, the financial office claimed never to have received the funds. This concerned me. Sooner or later, some auditor would note the number of applications received by the graduate school and then not find any record that the fees for those applications had ever been turned in to the university financial office. Extended negotiations with the people in the financial office failed to resolve the problem. They claimed they didn't have time to add up the checks and give us a receipt when we brought them over. It was a stalemate that left me seriously exposed to a negative audit, even though the money was being "lost" (i.e., assigned to some other account) at the other end of the line. The accountants were comfortable with that arrangement, but I was not.

There is an old saying that if you can't raise the drawbridge, lower the river. That, in effect, was the solution here. I managed to convince the upper administration that we should abandon the application fee in the interest of encouraging more applications, particularly from disadvantaged students. This was an instance where the solution to one problem became a plus on other grounds, since I truly believed in encouraging more applications in this way.

With no funds coming into the graduate office from outside, part of our problem with unreliable financial records was solved. There remained only the need to read each month's budget statement carefully. After monthly calls to the financial office protesting the misallocation of a thousand here or ten thousand there, the number of errors in our accounts dropped off, although I could never take their accuracy for granted. New administrators should remember that just because something appears in a computer printout doesn't mean that it's correct. Computers seldom lie, but sloppy bookkeeping can be entered into computers. It is another instance of the GIGO (garbage in, garbage out) principle.

Know the Whole Budget

Generally, a department's budget will be assigned by the dean of the college from the college's budget, which is allocated by the academic vice president or provost from the university's budget. A dutiful department chair or dean might accept the allocation without question (after, of course, pleading for more). This might not be the best policy. A unit administrator should try to have some understanding of all the budgeting of the university, difficult as this may be. This knowledge, properly used, may help to assure fairer distribution of the university's resources. At the least, it helps the administrator avoid being hood-winked by budgetary double-talk.

For example, there is the use of indirect costs charged for sponsored research projects, often a substantial amount at research universities. Indirect costs are generally a percentage of the direct costs granted for a given project. Thus if the grant for direct costs of a research project (equipment, materials, salaries, other direct expenses) is for $100,000, and if the negotiated indirect cost rate is 20% (this varies from 0% to 100%), then the indirect cost amount would be an additional $20,000. The negotiated percentage is usually based on quite specific categories of indirect costs: additional demands on the university library system, additional administrative time spent on the project, additional clerical demands for record keeping and report preparation, costs of maintaining office and laboratory space used for the project (heat, lights, telephones, computer systems, building cleaning and maintenance, etc.). All of these costs are laid out and a portion of the indirect cost charge is assigned to each. Generally, in my experience, these assignments are fairly reasonable and genuinely represent costs.

The problem lies in how the university uses the funds. I have too often seen those funds treated as if they were free money, new additions to the budget, to be spent in any way the controlling administrator sees fit. When this happens, the actual indirect costs that the funds were meant to cover must be met from some other budget. That other budget has, in my experience, turned out to be the resident instruction budget. Such an arrangement is unfair to the students of the university and to the teaching faculty.

Sometimes this subterfuge is disguised in intricate budgeting patterns. One time in my experience, it involved the budget allocations for the university library. The allocation formula was an elaborate complex of weighted factors, including such things as student credit hours produced, by level (lower division, upper division, master's level, doctoral level), grant research activity, number of faculty, number of degrees awarded, by level, and so on. I complained for some years that the formula discriminated against the arts and humanities by counting some research factors two or three different ways. I was always told that the advantages of the grant research-oriented departments were a reflection of their contribution of indirect cost funds. My response was that indirect cost money for library costs should be assigned directly to those areas that generate them and not be used vaguely for a patently biased budgeting formula. Finally, the library council agreed to do exactly that. To their surprise, as the chair of the council told me later, the result was a significant reduction of the library funds allocated to the research-oriented departments. The lesson here is that budgeting formulas should be kept as simple, direct, and transparent as possible.

The soft money of research sponsorship can create other traps for the unwary. A department that is highly successful in attracting research grants may expand its faculty accordingly. Then, when some of the grant sources dry up, that department may ask for additional resident instruction funds to keep the faculty formerly on the grant money. The problem again becomes the dreaded zero-sum. Some other department or departments will come up short if they are given additional resident instruction positions not justified by their teaching load. Departments that depend excessively on soft money may, in effect, ask the rest of the university to pull their irons out of the fire when hard times arrive. This might be the neighborly thing to do to a limited extent, but in all my years on research university campuses, not once did those departments offer to share their research wealth with the rest of us during the prosperous research grant years. Only during the lean years did sharing become their theme.

Other games can be played with budgets, of course. I recall a year in which my university's football program developed a serious deficit (not only in the won-lost columns but also in the budget). A colleague from the other large state university commented that we were showing a bigger football deficit than they were only because our accountants were not as creative as theirs. Our accountants, or more accurately our upper administration, soon became more creative. Assistant coaches began to show up on the resident instruction payroll, even though they were not teaching any classes. The athletic department's laundry bill disappeared but the physical education department's laundry bill (again a resident instruction budget item) expanded drastically. And so on. The resident instruction budget was being bled to bolster the intercollegiate athletics program.

In dealing with salary allocations, a new administrator must beware of the percentage trap. Remember that percentages are always based on an existing number. To use an extreme example, let us suppose that the average faculty salary in the engineering college is $60,000 and that the average in arts and humanities is $30,000. The dean of arts and humanities makes an appeal for greater equity to the academic vice president, who allocates salary funds. The vice president acknowledges that there is a problem and promises to begin correcting it. His solution is to grant 4% raises to the engineers and 6% raises to the faculty in arts and humanities. The arts and humanities dean may believe that progress is being made in closing the salary gap between the two groups, but that is not the case, because 4% of $60,000 is $2,400; 6% of $30,000 is $1,800. The gap has grown wider. Equity adjustments should not be based on percentages but on absolute numbers.

Percentage patterns can offer other problems, and sometimes opportunities. For example, one year as a department chair I had to hire an unusually large number of new faculty. These positions were authorized at the entry level, normally a new Ph.D. as an assistant professor. However, recruiting at that time, when there were more open positions than there were new Ph.D.s, often required dealing with graduate students who were presumably in their final dissertation year in graduate school. As a result, we could not be absolutely sure that our new faculty member would have completed the dissertation and the degree by the time she or he joined us. We customarily offered the rank of instructor and a lower salary if the degree had not been completed by the start of employment, and an assistant professorship and a higher salary if the degree had been completed.

I proposed to our dean that I be allowed to offer the same salary, whether or not the degree was completed, with the understanding that there would be no salary increase in succeeding years until the degree was in hand. I argued that this would simplify budget planning for the coming year because we would not have to wait until the beginning of the year to know what several of our new salaries would be. The dean accepted my proposal, and for years I continued using it in hiring.

Two advantages helped our department under this system. First, of course, our new faculty who had not completed their degree work received a higher salary in their first year, a matter of some importance to young faculty just coming out of graduate study. Second, all of the other members of the department benefited the following year due to using percentages in allocating salary money. This occurred because the department was allocated salary money in a lump sum based on the total salary budget of the previous year plus the percentage increase. By establishing higher salaries for the previous year's new positions, the department would get a higher allocation of salary money for the following year. If the new instructors did not receive a salary increase for the following year, but their salary lines generated additional money, that meant more money for the salaries of the rest of the faculty while, at the same time, keeping the new faculty of the previous year at or above what they might otherwise have received. We all came out ahead.

Not unexpectedly, the chronic malcontents in the department, who regularly invoked the open records law to examine the salaries of their colleagues, complained bitterly that new instructors were being paid assistant professor's salaries. I tried to explain to them why everyone in the department benefited from the practice, but they could not understand how that worked. I was concerned they would grumble loudly enough to alert the rest of the campus to the system and we would have to go back to the old pattern, but I don't think they ever understood it well enough to describe it to anyone outside the department.

The lesson here is to pay attention to the way percentages work. Sometimes they can help and sometimes they can hurt.

Student Credit Hours

For most state universities, student credit hours have become legal tender. They drive budgets for resident instruction, for faculty positions, and for new facility construction. There is a logic in this that appeals to state councils of higher education (or regents, or trustees, or whatever their title), and to legislative budget committees. It assumes that the human and material resources needed to teach students should be directly proportional, at any given time, to the number of students to be taught at that time. This assumption has an appealing logical simplicity, and the advent of computer data systems has made it even more attractive. With such systems, a higher education council with offices in the state capitol can determine, at any given hour on any given day, just how many student bottoms are in classroom seats on a specific campus. It may even tell them which seats. It leads to an industrial production model for higher education. In a sausage factory, if you know how many sausages are to be produced, you can easily calculate how much casing and how many pounds of meat must be provided. Unfortunately, the teaching of students, at any level, does not work like a sausage factory.

For example, if enrollment—either total for the university or in any given department—drops 100 students or so, it is difficult to dismiss a faculty member for one semester, or one year, and expect to hire that person back the following year. Universities do some such maneuvers with temporary appointments, but these appointments are often unfair to the temporaries. They cannot develop proper academic careers under these circumstances, and they cannot participate, as faculty members should, in the development of courses and curricula. So many of the stronger scholars will either go elsewhere to teach or give up teaching altogether. And yet, university budgets may oscillate widely if enrollment changes by even a hundred or two out of thousands. On the other hand, increased applications for admission by clearly qualified students can help a university's budget somewhat, but can stress faculty and physical resources to the point of lowering educational standards. Fully qualified, high-quality faculty cannot always be hired on short notice, nor can classrooms and laboratories be constructed overnight. Faced with such increased demand, universities and colleges may be put under considerable social and political pressure to expand.

Faced with this type of ad hoc budget making, universities have come to place a premium on getting and retaining students, whether or not those students belong at a university. Demographics vary with generations, so that the population of potential college students will vary. Social, economic, and political conditions will vary from year to year, making a college education seem more or less attractive to potential students. As a result, in those years in which there are high numbers of applications for college admission, universities can apply high standards for admission, and boast about their elite requirements. But when the number of applications drops, admission offices simply run their scale downward, adjusting their requirements to assure that the requisite number of students will be admitted.

Such a sliding scale can create all sorts of problems. Do we need to know the year a degree was awarded and the year when that graduate was admitted before we can judge the quality of the degree and the probable ability of the student? Are we to assume that there are no real standards to determine whether or not a student is capable of university-level work? Should faculty be issued a conversion factor each year to let them know how to set their standards in their courses? If you have high standards for seniors but should lower them for juniors, how do you handle a class that includes both juniors and seniors?

There is also the question of fairness to the applicants. There are many good and worthy people of value to our society who should not go to a university. They should perhaps study at a technical institute or a community college and prepare for careers that are not so academically oriented. I have seen a number of young people who would have been excellent machinists or welders who instead became mediocre— and not terribly happy—engineers. Good machinists and welders are as vital to our economy as are engineers. We need people who are good at what they do. People who like what they do tend more often to be good at it. Admitting a student who lacks aptitude for academic work may be as damaging to that student's future happiness as it is to the university's academic standards.

This use of a sliding scale for admissions has consequences beyond the individual campus. When the elite university in a region has lots of applicants and so can take only the very best, the second-tier universities can attract the best of the rejects, giving them some quite respectable students. When the elite university begins to slide its scale downward in lean years, it will skim off a much higher percentage of students genuinely capable of university-level work. The second-tier universities, in turn, will have to slide their scales downward. In such years, it sometimes seems as if the second-tier institutions are taking all those who can find their way to the campus, or who can get someone to take them there.

Retention of students can also become a serious problem under these circumstances. If a student flunks out, or just decides to leave, one more new admission is required to keep the budget up to par. Accordingly, great efforts and considerable resources are expended to keep students in school. It can become almost impossible for a student to fail, regardless of how ill-prepared, how unmotivated, or how academically incapable the student may be.

In my experience, lack of motivation has been the chief problem. Students with no interest in their studies, with little desire to learn, with no career goals or sense that they will ever have to support themselves or in any way be responsible for their own lives, present a real challenge. More importantly, they have no curiosity about themselves, their society, their culture, or the world in general. Such students are often at the university simply because their parents will continue to support them so long as they are in school. If they leave, they might have to go to work. For as long as they can stay in school (sometimes five or six or more years), they enjoy an active social life, party regularly, and avoid any significant personal responsibility.

Not only do they have such Edenic bliss, but as soon as their grades plummet, they have all sorts of counselors, tutors, advisors, mentors, people who constantly tell them how important they are to the university and what fine human beings they are altogether. Such support for the stumbling student is commendable, but one cannot help but wonder 1) how much of the university's resources should be diverted to such efforts rather than to library collections, faculty positions, and laboratory equipment and supplies that will help provide the capable and motivated students with a high-quality education, and 2) how many second chances should a manifestly unmotivated student be given? To look at this question from the student's side, how much could we reduce tuition and fees if we had a less elaborate system of student services? Such support services are nice, but they cost money, time, and space. Not all students need them, but all students help pay for them. Having worked with academic standards committees, I have observed that a year or two in what the counselors charmingly call "the world of work" often enhances a failing student's motivation to succeed upon returning to the university. If nothing else, the student has a little longer to grow up and assume some responsibility for his or her future.

Of course, there are other ways, in the short term, to keep student credit-hour production and head counts up to snuff. On one occasion, the university president partially made up for a shortfall by requiring all deans and directors to enroll in a computer basics course—one hour of credit, pass/fail. The class, of course, was a joke, but the credit hours and head count that were generated helped the university meet its budget.

If a university has a large graduate program, particularly if research assistantships are paying the tuition, directed studies can be useful to pad the credit-hour total. I have encountered one department in the applied biological sciences that used this subterfuge with reckless abandon. Master's degree candidates were accumulating numbers of credit hours similar to, or greater than, those normally required of doctoral studies. Students were required to do the manual labor needed in the maintenance of the research greenhouses, and they were paid not with money but with directed studies credit hours, over and above the students' normal programs of study. Some graduate students were forced to remain in their study program for a full year longer than necessary, in effect delaying their careers by a year, which resulted in a significant human cost. I asked the department chair about this practice, and he laughingly said that it was easier to keep experienced research assistants an extra year than to train new ones. It was a neat arrangement, if you are not worried about ethics. Research assistantships generated tuition money for the students, and the phony student credit hours attracted state resident instruction funding, all for the same activity. In a sense, the department was paid twice, did no teaching for it, and got some of their needed manual labor for free.

Such exploitation of graduate students is simply a part of the broader complex of considering graduate students primarily as a source of cheap skilled labor. A graduate research assistant comes very near to being an indentured servant paid at a much lower rate than the student's skills would command outside the university. Once a student has committed to a graduate program, it is very costly for him or her to leave and be admitted to some other program at another university. The new university will want recommendations from the former school, and a few negative words from that source can slam the door to further opportunities. Thus some programs are like the Mafia: Once in, you cannot leave without permission. If you do, you may be dead professionally. I recall the dean of one college of an applied science laughingly telling me that it was only a coincidence that the number of students admitted to his graduate programs always corresponded exactly with the number of research assistantships available.

My point is that the systems of relating dollars to student credit hour production need to be more sophisticated than they often are. A university is not a sausage factory, and its product is not simply student credit hours. Term-by-term fluctuations in enrollment should not cause term-by-term fluctuations in budget. A university needs more stability in its funding, and ethical stewardship in how it is administered. Resident instruction funding should certainly be related to enrollment, but over longer term averages. You cannot turn a university's activities up and down, like a water tap, and expect to have high-quality programs.

Outside Funding

Funding is a problem at most universities to the extent that some administrators are tempted to stretch their standards excessively. On one occasion, I was told by my dean that we were being offered an endowed professorship. That seemed like very good news indeed, until I learned the terms of the endowment. It seemed that a young assistant professor at another institution was being dismissed (he was not tenured) because of a reduction of the faculty. The young man's wealthy uncle was offering to endow a professorship in our department on the condition that we install his nephew as the endowed professor. My response was that we would be very happy to have the endowment and would name the chair after the uncle, but we would fill the position in our regular way—a national search and selection of the best-qualified candidate. This search would include the rules of affirmative action. The nephew, of course, could be one of the applicants.

This was not acceptable to the uncle. When another department heard of the situation, they informed the uncle that they would be happy to accept the endowment on the uncle's terms and welcome the nephew to their faculty, even though theirs was not the nephew's field. Dollars can speak very loudly. Fortunately, someone in the upper administration apparently decided that faculty positions should not be for sale and the deal was never consummated.

Research dollars from contracts and grants can present similar temptations. The research can be a major benefit to a university and should be encouraged. I have already suggested some of the problems that can arise from allocation of indirect cost money and use of graduate student time.

One can, from time to time, encounter entrepreneurial researchers, adept generators of grants and contracts who profess to have no particular obligation to the university or its students. They are under the impression that they support themselves entirely through their own efforts, benefiting the university more than the university benefits them. Too often, like so many football programs, they are merely the beneficiaries of creative bookkeeping and misallocation of funds. For instance, not all contracts and grants pay full indirect costs. And most contracts and grants could not have been attracted had the university not been there to host them. Buildings, services, and other resources, including the cheap labor of graduate research assistants, would not have been available had the university not existed. To put it baldly, the researcher needs the university more than the university needs that individual researcher. The researcher who feels no concern for the well-being of the university is acting against his or her own best interests. This is sometimes a difficult message to convey, but it should be offered as often as it is needed.

Entrepreneurial researchers who believe they are supporting the university will argue that their attraction of thousands or even millions of dollars to the university has a trickle-down effect on those areas of the university that do not attract large research grants. It is true that their efforts do have some benefits for the rest of the university—support for graduate students, purchase of equipment that can later be available to the educational program, and so on. But careful analysis of resources will often show that these researchers also drain away resources that might have gone to educational activities. The balance varies with the nature of the research, the indirect cost allowances, and how the funds are managed. Still, areas such as the humanities, which cannot expect large-scale grant support, actually benefit very little. As a colleague remarked when told he should be grateful for the benefits of the trickle-down effect, "I know all about trickle-down. I have been trickled-down on before."

The mindset of grant-getters can sometimes be intellectually narrow or even distorted. I was once invited to describe my then-current research project to a group of honors freshmen. I described the questions I was trying to answer, the problems I was encountering, and how I was trying to solve those problems. I wanted to give these especially bright students a sense of the stimulation and fun of doing research, and some sense of the value of the results. The next presentation, by a young engineering professor, only mentioned the subject of his research in passing. The burden of his message was how to get money through research grants. He very proudly related how, when one source of funding dried up, he simply changed how he described his research and what he called it (he did not change the research), so he could appeal to other possible sources. His criterion of research success was not in terms of new knowledge gained, but rather in terms of dollars attracted, by whatever stratagem. Shrewdness rather than intellectual inquiry was his key to success. Grantsmanship rather than insightful inquiry was the recommended skill. This was not an isolated instance. As I have observed before, many of the faculty, when asked how their research was progressing, would answer in terms of grant dollars attracted rather than research results gained.

Another set of problems can arise from the management of research results. I have heard of occasions when researchers were pressured to report the results the sponsor wanted, rather than the results actually achieved. The message was said to have been that the wrong results would assure that the researcher would receive no further funds from that source. Such pressures have been known to come not only from private sources, but also from politically sensitive government agencies. The researcher who yields to these pressures can design the research in such a way that the desired result is inevitable. The research data can simply be falsified, or portions of the research results can be omitted from the published reports. When such pressures are exerted, the university needs to stand fast and support the honest researcher in reporting the actual results.

The issues of classified research and proprietary research are more difficult. The scientific (and indeed the broader scholarly) tradition is one of sharing new knowledge freely, generally through journals and books. This enables review of results. Experiments can be replicated and the results verified. Other researchers can use the results to move on to further research and still greater understanding of our world. Government research related to national security and/or law enforcement certainly is important to all of us and obviously cannot always be made public. With the advent of the war on terrorism, even some research in the social sciences (history, psychology, political science) might need to be kept confidential, at least for a time, in the interest of public security. A university needs to consider its policies carefully on this sensitive point and review them regularly as conditions change.

Similar issues on perhaps a smaller scale, can arise with proprietary research. If a corporation or consortium of corporations provides the funds for a research program, the sponsor may wish to keep the results confidential so that its competitors cannot benefit from the work. To what extent should a university agree to such research, with restrictions on publication? Some universities have divisions separate from their academic function that are established specifically for such research. Some of these establishments have spun off into independent research institutes. Again, ethical and financial implications of such problems should be considered carefully and policies put in place so that the institution does not have to respond on a purely ad hoc basis in individual cases. If a large corporation is knocking on the door with a check for hundreds of thousands, or even millions, of dollars in its hand, the tempted administrator needs the guidance of already established, well-thought-out policies. With some guidance, Dr. Faustus might be restrained from selling his soul.

BRYANT'S FIFTEENTH LAW OF ACADEMIC ADMINISTRATION

Research grants should primarily serve the interests of the research, not the researcher or the grantor.

Allocations of Space

While the new administrator is learning to read financial budget and accounting documents, he or she should also learn to read accounts of other allocations of the university's resources. How is space being allocated? What is the availability of general equipment? And so on. To give an example, my university was beginning to experience a shortage of classrooms as enrollment increased. Members of the upper administration asked to meet with the dean and department chairs of our college to discuss offering more evening classes to ease the shortage. Before the meeting, I examined the printed class schedule for that term and the upcoming term.

After a vice president made a presentation exhorting us to increase our numbers of evening classes to help with the crisis, I asked a very simple question: How many evening classes were being offered by the other colleges? The answer, as I had already determined by looking at the class schedules, was none. I pointed out that our college already offered a substantial number of evening classes, and suggested that the other colleges should match our effort before we were asked to do more. The meeting was adjourned shortly thereafter without any commitment on our part to offer more evening classes.

Universities are sufficiently dynamic institutions that there may be frequent needs for remodeling existing space. As fields of study change, or as enrollment patterns change, offices may have to become classrooms, or classrooms may have to become laboratories, or laboratories may need new configurations to meet new developments. When these needs arise, in come the physical plant people with their cost estimates.

Sometimes these costs can be surprisingly high. Some years ago, my university found itself burdened with astonishingly high remodeling costs from the physical plant people, costs substantially above what one would expect to pay a commercial contractor. The physical plant people insisted that their higher costs were the result of much higher standards of quality. Watching them in action, many of us began to suspect that higher costs were paying for lower efficiency, errors, and perhaps some featherbedding. At the same time, there was an attitude that when the job was done, the paying department could take it or leave it. The physical plant people did not seem very interested in whether the work was done to the purchaser's satisfaction.

Complaints produced no improvement. Physical plant charges were siphoning off more and more of the university's resources that might otherwise have gone to other uses, such as laboratory supplies, travel expenses, and books for the library. The whole campus was being bled by a physical plant bureaucracy that showed no interest in efficiency or cost containment. Finally, the burden became so severe and disproportionate that the administration had to act. It declared that any remodeling work over a certain amount (I think it was $500) could be let out for bids from private contractors, in competition with the physical plant's estimate of costs. All jobs, from private contractors as well as physical plant staff, had to meet the same set of specifications, so quality of work was not a major issue.

The result was a precipitous drop in the number of jobs the physical plant people had to do, which meant a substantial drop in remodeling costs to the university. It also meant a significant drop in the number of employees working for the physical plant. After that, physical plant estimates became much more reasonable, and physical plant employees became much more eager to please the departments paying for the work. The real benefit, of course, was that a much smaller proportion of the university's resources was consumed by remodeling costs, leaving more for the real purposes of the university.

During periods of growth, a dean or department chair may be involved in the planning of new buildings. This can provide yet another set of challenges. Some architects have no experience with designing university buildings, some have had experience but have failed to learn from their mistakes, and some have learned well. Fortunate is the university that employs an architect who understands what an academic building needs to be and has learned from past mistakes.

If the architects, or the upper administration, are wise enough to consult the faculty and administrators who will actually use the building and pay attention to their comments, the process should be taken very seriously. Do not be overly impressed by artistic exterior elevations of the building, complete with purple trees that would have to be at least a 100 feet tall and people who would be perhaps 5 feet tall. Look at the plans room by room, corridor by corridor, closet by closet. Imagine as fully as you can the activity that is supposed to take place in each of those spaces. Consider if the spaces provided are the spaces that are really needed. Does the building feature classrooms holding 100 or more students, while your department or college generally offers classes of 20 to 30? Or vice versa? Are there enough seminar rooms for your graduate classes? Are there enough laboratories and are they of the right size and shape? Are they accessible for the equipment you need to move into them? Are they accessible to handicapped faculty and students? Even such apparently trivial details as the number and location of electrical outlets can have a large impact on the usefulness of a given classroom. It is an exercise in detailed visualization. It takes time and effort, but the price of failing to visualize accurately can be years of frustration and artificial, unnecessary limitations on the unit's activities, or expensive remodeling of a new building.

I have taught in classrooms that were extremely wide from side to side, and shallow from front to back. If I wanted to lecture, it was extremely difficult to make eye contact with the students at the far left and right. I had to speak more loudly than normal to be heard (hard on the students in the center), and chalkboard illustrations were difficult for the students at the sides to see. We could not turn the class 90 degrees for a narrow, deep classroom because one side wall was all windows and the other had the door in the center and no chalkboard. Class discussions were similarly disjointed because the students were spread so awkwardly that they could not always hear each other's comments. These were rooms that were designed from the first as classrooms, yet no sensible teacher would have approved that configuration. It is clear that the architect knew nothing about teaching, and teachers either were not consulted or they did not take the process seriously enough.

In another case, a science building was designed with two three-story wings connected by a one-story center section for offices. The architect's rendering of the exterior was very nice. The building was attractively symmetrical and looked impressive. Unfortunately, although elevator shafts were built in, no elevator was provided to take materials and equipment to laboratories on the second and third floors, and there was no access to those floors for disabled faculty and students. In addition, faculty and students on the third floor of one wing had to go down to the first floor and across and up again to get to the third floor of the other wing. The faculty put up with the problem until the Americans with Disabilities Act compelled them to put in elevators. By that time, the existing elevator shafts had been filled with ventilation ducts from the various laboratories. No provision for such ducts had been made in the original plans, even though the laboratories themselves were in the plans. So it was necessary to add new elevator shafts at the end of each wing, two shafts when one should have been sufficient. Even so, it was still a long way from the third floor of one wing to the third floor of the other. Some forethought of how that building was to be used would have avoided both the inconvenience and much of the added expense.

On another campus, a charming old building was profoundly remodeled. In effect, it was completely gutted and a new interior constructed in the old shell. The result included some very nice spaces, but it also included classrooms with large load-bearing columns in the middle of the room. The rated capacity of those rooms included student seats behind the columns, but, of course, that was impractical. The students could not see the instructor or the front of the room, and they could not hear much of what was being said. Those rooms were, in effect, an architectural swindle, providing the university with less real student capacity than had been bargained for. Any experienced teacher, indeed anyone, should have been able to point out the problem.

In another case, a group of designing architects became enamored of a curved facade on a new administration building. The exterior was esthetically pleasing, but the curved space in the interior created a great deal of wasted space because of curved outside walls that enclosed square, straight interior walls and square, straight furniture (and, I suppose, a certain number of square, straight people).

My offices were to be a part of that building. I found various difficulties, including an arrangement that put a large bank of frequently used file drawers directly in one of the main traffic passages in the office, assuring that people would regularly be blocked by open file drawers, both a nuisance and a hazard. In addition, although the computed square footage of the offices compared with the space we already occupied, the curved outside wall meant that the usable space would be considerably less. I asked that our office be dropped from the plan, and it was.

Every experienced teacher has probably had occasion to put up with bad acoustics, poor lighting, inadequate ventilation, and other physical obstacles to teaching and learning. Cost constraints do limit some of the refinements that might be desirable in the ideal classroom, but even on a limited budget, care and forethought and imaginative visualization of the activities to take place in new space can avoid the worst pitfalls of bad planning. No plan is ever perfect, but care and thought by faculty and administrators who will actually use new space is effort very well invested. Besides avoiding the worst errors, perhaps the architect might be educated about the functions of university buildings.

Never Enough

As a general rule, the administration and faculty of every university feel that they do not have enough resources. There may be a very few, extremely well-endowed private institutions who feel they have enough, but these are rare. Even those who feel they have enough may well plead poverty at budget time, in hopes of attracting just a bit more.

A former colleague of mine served for a number of years as vice president of a highly respected private liberal arts college in the upper Midwest. He told me the story of his first year, when he was asked to prepare the budget for the following year. The college was fairly well endowed. He went to work, analyzing, adjusting, trimming here to add there, and proudly presented a fully balanced budget to the college's long-time president, who would, in turn, present it to the governing board. The president looked at his budget and immediately concluded that his new vice president did not yet know how to make a budget. The president would have to revise it.

At the meeting of the governing board, which consisted of a group of wealthy alumni and other supporters of the college, the president presented his budget. In that budget, the needs of the college far out-stripped its resources. The president expatiated on the dire straits in which the college found itself and the severe consequences that would occur in face of the cuts needed to squeeze into the available resources. Finally, one of the board pulled out a checkbook and said, "All right. What do you need?" The others followed suit and soon the college was richer by a substantial amount. As they were leaving the meeting, the president said to the new vice president, "Now that's the way to write a budget."

Private schools look to donors. Public schools look to legislatures as well as donors. And all, to a greater or lesser extent, look to the federal government. All rely to some extent on tuition and fees from the students. None of those groups will ever hear a school saying, "We have plenty. No need to send more next year."

BRYANT'S SIXTEENTH LAW OF ACADEMIC ADMINISTRATION

No academic unit ever thinks it has enough resources.

To be fair, this is not simple greed. Both education and research are bottomless pits. There are always good and useful things that can be done with additional resources. Beyond reasonable minimums, the real question is how much can or will society provide for colleges and universities? In most cases, whatever society does provide will be a sound investment that will pay off handsomely in the long term. It is good to keep the pressure on society to provide as much as possible.

This pattern, however, may result in problems with faculty morale. If administrators constantly plead poverty and financial crisis to the faculty, and many do, faculty morale may decline, and many faculty, assuming their school's plight is unique, may try to move elsewhere. Certainly some universities have more resources than others, and one can understand a faculty member wanting to go where there are better-equipped laboratories, a better library, and higher faculty salaries. Unfortunately, some make the leap to a higher salary only to find that the increase is more than taken up by a much higher cost of living and greater inconvenience of living at the new institution.

Then, too, we should keep in mind the story of the boy who cried "Wolf!" once too often. The point for administrators is that care should be used in constantly announcing budget crises. Yes, more resources would be wonderful. Yes, you would like your faculty to have higher salaries. But the same is true at most other institutions. Sometimes giving more attention to getting the best possible use out of what you already have might be more productive.

In summary, a unit's administrator, whether department chair or dean, must be aware not only of the unit's resources and how they are being handled, but also of the broader university picture, and plans, to assure that her or his unit is being treated fairly and intelligently. In addition, an administrator should have a realistic sense of the difference between unlimited, ideal resources and workable, limited resources within the constraints of what society is able and willing to provide.

BRYANT'S SEVENTEENTH LAW OF ACADEMIC ADMINISTRATION

When you are told how big a piece of the resources pie
your unit is getting, try to find out where
the rest of the pie is going and why.

8 WHAT IS A UNIVERSITY? OR, WHAT SHOULD IT BE?

A University should be a place of light, of liberty, and of learning.

—Benjamin Disraeli

It is a great point then to enlarge the range of studies which a University professes, even for the sake of the students: and, though they cannot pursue every subject which is open to them, they will be the gainers by living among those and under those who represent the whole circle.

—John Henry Cardinal Newman

Ultimately, an administrator's behavior should be based on a vision of what a university should and should not be. I have very seldom heard any administrator articulate a broad concept of what a university is or should be, but there must be at least a tacit vision underlying our approach to our work. This can range from seeing the university merely as a place to get a good job, to the most high-flown idealism about service to humanity. In addition to what I said in the

Prologue, let me try to articulate my concept of what a university should, and should not, be.

A university should preserve existing knowledge, generate new knowledge, and transmit its knowledge to any who desire it. It should provide a place for the free exchange of ideas, and the free examination and competition of disparate ideas. All the knowledge we think we have should be open to examination and verification. This can be irritating at times, as when some faculty become professional iconoclasts delighting in being as outrageous as possible, with no sense of intellectual integrity or responsibility. This, however, is the price we must pay to keep the university an open marketplace of ideas.

A primary goal of a university in our democracy should be to prepare citizens to take an informed, responsible role in the governance of the nation. This means they must know the democratic traditions underlying our form of government and understand how that government works. University graduates, regardless of their field of study, should be able to provide leadership that strengthens our democratic form of governance. This does not mean that they must seek office, necessarily, but that they should be informed participants in the life and governance of their communities.

When I can ask a university class of 40 students what is meant by a government of laws and not of men (and, of course, of women), or ask them what is meant in legal proceedings by a bill of particulars, and no one has the slightest idea of either, it is clear that students are not prepared to participate intelligently in maintaining our democratic traditions. When these same students neither understand what the ad hominem fallacy is, nor recognize such a fallacy when they encounter one, they are obviously not prepared to judge wisely between two political candidates for office. University students should not be allowed to graduate in such a state of ignorance, whether or not they can design a highway or a computer or a petrochemical plant, teach a third grade class, or perform in Carnegie Hall.

The ideal of the university as an open marketplace of ideas and a preparer of informed citizenry is easy to say, but extremely difficult to achieve, or even approximate, because of social, political, economic, and just plain human pressures to the contrary. Working toward the ideal might be easier if we keep in mind some of the things a university should not be.

A university should not be merely a safe haven/sinecure for those who use their facility with things academic to escape the challenges and responsibilities of the world. Administrators, faculty, and students all have a responsibility to the society that created and supports the university. That responsibility includes intellectual integrity, energetic pursuit of knowledge, transmission of that knowledge, and the ethical use of that knowledge for the benefit of society.

A university should not simply be a training school for specific jobs. Turning out neatly shaped parts to fit into the giant machines of corporate enterprise is not the basic function of a university. As a general rule, an educated person will be of greater value to any enterprise than an ignorant person, but vocational training should be secondary to liberal education. University graduates must be prepared as enlightened citizens in a free society, not just as specialized drones in busy hives controlled by queen bees and soldiers. Corporate leaders like to emphasize how rapidly our society constantly changes, but these same leaders ask our universities to train students to fill today's subordinate jobs. A university career normally takes at least four years to complete, by which time, if the corporate leaders are to be believed, those jobs will be obsolete, or at least obsolescent. Universities should not be a party to such blatant contradiction. Nor should universities be a party to the subordination of bright young minds to the desires of corporate executives.

In particular, programs for preparing professional educators should not be restricted to the narrow techniques and bureaucratic paraphernalia of the field. For example, a doctoral candidate where I once worked was given a preliminary examination (multiple choice at the doctoral level!) of his general cultural knowledge. On one question, he told me afterward, he was asked to identify Moby Dick. He said he could eliminate three of the choices easily, but finally was unsure whether it was a white whale or a brown bear. He chose the brown bear. Once he completed his degree, this man expected to become a school principal, or perhaps a district superintendent. I submit that the university had failed both this man and the public school system, on the ground that a director of the education of our young people should have a broad knowledge of American culture and traditions. His ignorance of this particular fact was only a trivial indicator of his broader deficiency in such knowledge.

At another university, I found that the doctoral candidates in a field of science were not qualified to teach the freshman course in that science because their own undergraduate studies had been so narrowly specialized. Some of their professors had a similar problem and freely admitted it.

A university should not be a mere purveyor of information. Information is available in great quantities from many sources without the trouble and expense of attending a university. Rather, a university should help a student decide what information to seek, how to seek it, and how to use that information to construct ideas and develop understanding.

A university should not be a mere retailer of credits, certificates, and degrees. Although most students do pay tuition, they are not "customers" who must be entertained, and who pick and choose what (or even whether) to study and what they prefer not to know. Students, after all, can hardly judge the value of knowledge that they have not yet acquired. Faculty advisers are all too familiar with students who want to be concert pianists or neurosurgeons, but who do not want to practice scales or study anatomy. Like the abortive graduate director described in Chapter 5, they want the prestige and privileges of such positions without the rigorous efforts and significant achievements required.

A university educational experience and the intellectual development it should provide cannot be gained solely through electronic means. Distance learning is not university learning. An effective teacher, in a live classroom, will be constantly aware of the students, particularly how they are responding to whatever is happening in the classroom. The responses of students to questions and discussion, their manner, tone, and body language, and everything happening in the room can provide perceptive teachers with clues about how well the students are responding and learning. Such a teacher will adjust the presentation according to what those clues are saying. As a child, I attended a Methodist church whose pastor came from the southern tradition of the eloquent pulpit oratory made nationally prominent by Dr. Martin Luther King, Jr. Our minister was a fine preacher who could often move his congregation profoundly, but sometimes, for whatever reason, the spark did not reach the congregation. The preacher, always sensitive to his congregation, would on such occasions abruptly interrupt himself in mid-sermon and call for the singing of a hymn. The organist, in turn, knew the trick of modulating to the next higher key for the second verse. Thus invigorated, the congregation was awake and ready to hear, understand, and be moved by the rest of the sermon.

Teachers usually cannot have their classes sing hymns, but they can shift gears in mid-class, so to speak. If a lecture is falling flat, stop talking and start asking questions. If the questioning reveals something the students have not understood, go back over that material in some other way. Do something different. Do not just plow doggedly on with a presentation that is not working. This kind of sensitivity and ability to adapt is severely limited or, for the most part, absent from distance learning techniques. There is little or no opportunity for the kind of subtle sensitivity to students that makes a great teacher.

Universities should use the most advanced communication technology when that technology affords advantages. Certainly a video conference or videotape of a world-renowned artist or scientist or historian can be a valuable experience for a student. The danger lies in becoming so enamored of the latest dazzling technological tricks that we forget to consider their value for our purposes. I worked in a state that had, at great expense, constructed a distance learning system using a satellite. This meant building expensive uplinks at a limited number of institutions and purchasing expensive satellite time when a signal was to be broadcast. The system was expensive and wasteful because the satellite's "footprint" was much larger than the state that sponsored the broadcast. For the costs involved in presenting a course, several competent instructors might have been hired to present the material in person, or fellowships could have been provided to make it possible for all participants to go to the originating university campus for study.

Proponents of distance learning argue that the system makes it possible to offer the expertise of an outstanding authority on a subject to a widely dispersed audience. They make the very valid point that such an authority, on a television screen, may be more stimulating intellectually than a much less qualified instructor who is live in the classroom. They are correct, as far as their argument goes. If a world authority can be put on the TV screen, by all means do so, but there needs to be a competent instructor live in the classroom, also. There is no substitute for the engaged human presence. Unfortunately, after advocates of distance learning have made their world authority argument, they proceed to present courses that use ordinary, run of the mill faculty as instructors. Their argument and their practice do not coincide.

Telecommunication techniques of distance learning are of great value to a university as a way to update practicing professionals and to enrich other programs, and they should be encouraged for those uses. But they most emphatically should not be regarded as a valid way to provide something called a university education. A genuine university experience of the kind I have tried to describe cannot be mediated through a video display or by any other purely electronic means. Data can be transmitted electronically. Ideas can be described through electronic means. But a dynamic intellectual community cannot be fully established remotely. You have to be there and be actively engaged.

I once worked for a dean of engineering who liked to make a distinction between education and training. Education had to do with breadth of vision, flexible habits of mind, the ability to solve problems innovatively, an understanding of consequences, and the ability to fit one's actions into broader social contexts. Training, on the other hand, was more focused on learning to do certain tasks, mastering specific techniques and bodies of data, and gaining narrowly developed and highly specialized skills. Distance learning, it seems to me, is very useful for training but of limited use in education.

There are other sidetracks to what I would consider a genuine university education, some of them very attractive. Almost everyone would agree that a university education should be an experience that goes beyond attending classes and taking notes and examinations. The student services people insist that this additional experience should be social, but that misses the mark. When students have told me that their primary reason for coming to the university was to meet people from a variety of backgrounds, I have advised them to join the military. There they will meet and interact with people from more widely varied backgrounds than they are likely to encounter at a university.

This is not to say that the university experience does not involve interaction with others. Such interaction is, or should be, at the core of the experience, but it should be more intellectual than social. Students should have the opportunity to interact, outside of classes, with their professors and with other students. As a student I learned a great deal in informal conversation, over coffee, with faculty and other students. What I learned was not so much facts or data as it was habits of mind, angles of vision, ways of being intellectually engaged with a subject. Often these conversations were with students and faculty from other fields of study, opening my intellectual horizons still further. This is the kind of intellectual community that attendance at a genuine university can provide. Such an experience is not available through distance learning or teleconferencing. You have to be there. It is also not available at keggers on the fraternity lawn on a beautiful spring night. That is education of a sort that is not peculiar to universities.

What distinguishes a university from a college and a college from a community college? In recent years there has been a pattern of aspiration that has seen community colleges trying to become four-year colleges, and a great many four-year colleges have thought that by changing their name to university they could actually become universities. What are the differences?

The distinctions have become blurred, of course. Basically, a community college offers two-year programs of vocational training as well as the first two years of baccalaureate study. A four-year college offers the baccalaureate degree. Some also offer a limited number of master's degrees or other specialized five-year programs. Universities offer not only the baccalaureate but also advanced degrees, usually through the doctorate. Another distinction is that a genuine university includes a strong component of research and creative activity beyond that found at most colleges.

One implication of these distinctions is that a university will offer a more cosmopolitan intellectual atmosphere, and ideally, more interaction between what is taught in the classroom and what is happening on the cutting edge of research. In addition, one expects to find a more distinguished faculty at a university, although this is not always so.

In practice, many universities have become megaversities, chillingly impersonal and little concerned with undergraduate students. A common complaint at such institutions is that many of the freshman and sophomore courses are taught by graduate assistants who are themselves students at a higher level and who are relatively inexperienced. They work cheap but do not offer the level of knowledge and distinction of the senior faculty, whose reputation might have attracted the undergraduate students to that campus.

This may be a weakness, particularly if the graduate assistants are not properly supervised. However, there are arguments to justify the situation. On the matter of the level of qualification of the graduate assistants, we should remember that they generally have at least as many credentials as a lot of the instructors at community colleges. The only difference is that they are trying to gain additional credentials. Every teacher at one time is a beginning teacher.

Most of the institutions that call themselves universities fall far short of being an ideal community of scholars. Such a community may develop within individual departments, but even then it is not guaranteed. Narrow self-interest too often will get in the way. Salary increases, office or laboratory space, promotions, course assignments, and a host of other factors can create an air of competition and rivalry rather than of community. I have even known faculty to measure relative status by the proximity of their offices to the department office. On the other hand, a good friend who once got caught quite innocently in a war between the department chair who hired him and the dean of his college, and who lost his job as a result, concluded that a certain level of anonymity on campus was desirable. When he encountered his dean walking on campus, he wanted the dean to recognize that he was a member of that dean's faculty, but he did not want the dean to know his name. Such a delicate balance might be helped by having one's office farther away from the department office, and quite far from the dean's office.

I don't have a clear answer to this problem. The closest I have been able to come is to try to minimize the areas of friction. If decisions concerning such matters as salary and course assignments are made openly on the basis of established criteria agreed to by the majority of the faculty, most faculty members will accept the results as fair. Established procedures and openness in their application can do much to slow the rumor mill and inhibit the conspiracy theorists.

An ideal university, then, is an intellectual community of learners and teachers who continue to learn. It is a place of inquiry and debate, an open forum for questions, ideas, beliefs, and knowledge. As I have already suggested, every form of unenlightened self-interest, selfishness, shortsightedness, and downright foolishness that can be found in any group of humans can be found on a university campus. These traits keep the university from achieving the ideal of a genuine intellectual community of scholars. But sometimes a university can come close. Part of the job of any university administrator should be to do what can be done to realize this ideal.

9   WHO SHOULD GOVERN A UNIVERSITY?

*He that goeth about to persuade a multitude, that they
are not so well governed as they ought to be, shall never
want attentive and favourable hearers.*

—Richard Hooker

*The people's government, made for the people, made by
the people, and answerable to the people.*

—Daniel Webster

"Who is in charge here?" was the rather plaintive question of
a long-time university president when student unrest broke
out on his campus. He thought he was. The faculty, through their
faculty council, thought they were. The students claimed they should
be in charge and fully intended to take over. In the background was a
governing board who thought that they had some considerable say in
the university's affairs. Off in the capital city there were legislators who
considered themselves the final arbiters in the affairs of a state university, even to the point of micromanaging membership on the faculty,
admission, and programs to be offered. So who should be in charge?
A conscientious administrator should consider this question with care

and then work toward the form of governance that will best move the institution toward the ideal.

All of the groups just mentioned have some influence on the university, of course. Governance of a university becomes a matter of collaboration and negotiation at many different levels. The administrator who expects to make unilateral decisions without sensitivity to these needs for collaboration is destined for a bumpy road that eventually leads out the door, or at least out of the administrative office and back to the classroom full-time. But again, as with the idea of what a university should be, an administrator should have some ideal paradigm of how a university should be governed, and on what principles. Who should be making which decisions?

Most faculty members will say that a university should be run democratically, but of course their demos will usually include only the faculty. I have encountered a case in which even administrators who also held faculty appointments were denied the vote in such governance. The result was that administrators regularly found ways to circumvent faculty governance, and faculty governance often made ill-informed and often purely self-serving decisions.

Some administrators feel that their greater access to relevant information, their full-time or nearly full-time focus on the conduct of the university, and (please don't smile) their greater objectivity should make it obvious that they need to have control of decision-making.

Students will agree with faculty that governance should be democratic, but of course many of them will identify the "people" of their democratic governance as the students, excluding faculty, staff, and administration. They regard themselves as the customers, and the customer is always right.

On many campuses, very quietly and without any public declarations, the secretaries, administrative assistants, nonacademic directors, and other support staff actually run most things. But perhaps we should not explore that underground governance (which can be very efficient) for fear of disrupting it and throwing some universities into chaos.

Whichever group (administrators, faculty, staff, students, politicians) is finally in charge, it will sooner or later settle into a pattern of governing for its own benefit. That is axiomatic in American democracy: life, liberty, and the pursuit of happiness; government of the people, by the people, and for the people. This is the strength (and sometimes the weakness) of democracy: If the government is for the people, presumably the people will conduct it in their own best interests. Government by the people will be conducted for the people who govern. So the question becomes one of what group the university is intended to serve and to benefit. If we can identify that group, then it, or its representatives, should be in charge.

In one way or another, the university benefits students, staff, faculty, and administration, and of course its ultimate purpose is to benefit society. An obvious purpose for the university is to provide an advanced education for those students who are able to benefit from it. As I have already suggested, however, students, especially young students, are not competent to judge what they do not yet know. Further, there are many students who regard the university not primarily as a source of education, but rather as a haven from leaving the support of their parents and getting a job, or as a great social opportunity to party, or as a source of easily gained certification that will magically give them good jobs and lots of money. So perhaps students should be part of the "people" in the democratic conduct of the university because its purpose is to a great extent to benefit them, but they should not have final control. One requisite of a viable democracy is an intelligent and informed electorate. The students may be intelligent, but they are not yet informed. That is why they should be at the university in the first place, to become informed.

The university serves the faculty by allowing them to teach those things that they care about and are informed about, and to engage in advanced research to extend our knowledge. On the other hand, it may be seen as a haven from accountability, as a sinecure, and as a base from which to obtain generous research grants. Faculty have been known to make decisions about curriculum and course offerings that are not in the best interests of the students, but instead accommodate faculty interests and convenience. They have even constructed curricula designed to protect faculty positions. I recall an instance in which a department proposed a curriculum with only three hours of elective in an entire four-year curriculum, and those hours came in the senior year. All the rest of the curriculum was prescribed, semester by semester, through the four years. The faculty council approved the plan because the members knew that if they opposed it, the college from which it came would oppose any curricular proposals the others might bring to the council. It was a shameful performance, but it did happen, and there have been many other instances which, though less egregious, were clearly based on faculty interest rather than good educational policy. So faculty have an interest in being part of the mix, but perhaps should not be trusted with total control. As with the students, the faculty are a part of the people who are to benefit from university governance, but they are not all.

Many of the staff take genuine satisfaction in their role of supporting the university's function of educating students and advancing human knowledge. But again there are the instances, such as I have suggested in accounting practices and physical plant construction projects, in which shortsighted self-interest seems to get in the way of serving university purposes. And, too, staff don't often have the knowledge necessary to make curricular and other educational decisions.

These are all constituencies that have some legitimate claim to a voice in the governance of a university, but none of them, nor all of them together, constitute all of the people embodied in the formula of government "for the people." The missing element, a large and essential one, is society itself. It is society that provides the majority of support for universities, that delegates important rights for certification (degrees, certificates, and licenses) to universities, and that allows universities to have many special privileges. In the broadest view, the mission of the university is to serve the needs of society. If society is both the primary support and the ultimate beneficiary of the university, that is, the people for whom the university works, then should the governance of the university be "of the people" and "by the people"?

There are problems with this somewhat simplistic paradigm. Some of these problems result from shortcomings by universities themselves. For example, a reasonable proportion of the legislators in most states have university degrees, and some have advanced degrees, including those in law, medicine, engineering, and business. Yet a great many of these legislators seem to have little or no sense of what a university is or how it operates. Some of this may be simply grandstanding to the voters, but much of it, I am persuaded, is genuine ignorance. The same phenomenon may be observed with members of Congress, governors, and other elected and appointed members of government, not to mention alumni/alumnae in general. How can this be?

Some public officials have not attended a university or are simply invincibly ignorant. The legislator who asked a distinguished university president in a committee hearing, "Where was you borned at?" or the one who questioned why a university museum spent $250 each for two brassieres when what had been purchased were two bronze braziers, art objects of considerably more value—such people are perhaps beyond the reach of any university effort. But that does not answer the basic question for university graduates.

How can reasonably intelligent and literate people spend four or more years at an institution of higher learning and come away with little idea of what that institution is or how it works? How can they believe, for example, that a 12-hour teaching load means that a professor only works 12 hours a week? How can they believe that a university is nothing more than a technical training school for specific jobs? Some of these failures can be blamed on the universities themselves. Seldom, if ever, is there any effort to explain the university to its students (or even to its faculty, for that matter). If we have reasonably intelligent people with us for four or more years and they leave with no accurate sense of who we are, what we do, how we do it, or why, we have not been very good teachers. If society is to play a role in our governance, we need to assure that it understands what it is governing. We need to have a clearer idea of who we are, and we need to explain ourselves better to our students and to society in general. This should be a continuing effort, generation after generation.

I do not have a pat formula for university governance. It is a complex subject that has not received enough consideration. All constituencies should have an effective voice. The strength of that voice should vary with the questions under consideration, but every constituency should have some voice in all matters, enough to ensure that no group's interest or effectiveness is sacrificed for the unilateral benefit of another. In particular, the voice of society should be better balanced and better informed. Society's voice should be represented not by a few political hacks appointed by the governor to pay off political debts (for public universities), nor by a few wealthy donors (for private universities). Society's representatives should have an understanding of the nature and function of a university and should believe in a university's mission. They should be joined, at the highest level, by representative voices for the faculty, the staff, the administration, and the students, to assure that all aspects of university life are kept in perspective. They should be people willing to spend more than a day or two each year keeping informed on university matters. They should not be people with specific political axes to grind. And they should not, as has been my experience in several instances, get their information about the university only through the university president and the president's representatives. I have seen university presidents manipulate governing boards shamelessly, sometimes to the disadvantage of the university community. This should not be allowed to occur.

BRYANT'S EIGHTEENTH LAW OF ACADEMIC ADMINISTRATION

Democracy is the ideal in governance, but it is important
to keep clear what exactly constitutes,
or should constitute, the demos.

Epilogue

U niversities have been jokingly characterized as a large number of departments bound together only by a search for adequate parking space. Certainly there are centrifugal forces that threaten to turn some universities into an anarchic hodgepodge, but those forces must be resisted if universities are to survive as universities. More accurately, and optimistically, universities might be likened to a large, complex organism, with each part in some way serving the whole as well as its own interests.

The humanists need the social scientists, the social scientists need the biologists, the biologists need the chemists, the chemists need the physicists, all the sciences and most of the social sciences need the mathematicians. Whether they know it or not, the whole lot need the philosophers, in particular the ethicists. So who needs the humanists? A colleague of mine once remarked that the role of the humanities at a research university was to keep the scientists "from being too damned sure." A worthy goal, but I would add that the humanities also should help all of us understand what it is to be human. What about the artists? I would say that they, too, can help us understand the nature of the human experience and perhaps inspire us to make it better.

All of these interdependent needs are what make the university necessary, what make it indeed a single organism with interdependent parts. Lose any one of these and you do not have a university. Isolate any one of these from the rest, and the insitution will eventually wither or grow excessively narrow and inbred. Inbreeding does finally produce idiots.

The task of the administrators is to hold all of these parts together in a way that allows all of them to make their proper contribution to the whole. The administrators are the glue that holds all those departments, and their parking lots, together in a functioning whole. They are the "stay against confusion." As the occasion dictates, they are the leaders or the enablers who help the faculty carry out their various missions. They handle the red tape, catch the flak, look for and organize the ways and means. They provide leadership, or at least coordination and coherence, in the development of new programs, new curricula, and new research directions. They assure standards of excellence in both education and research. They often provide crucial mediation among disparate faculty ideas.

There are no Nobel or Pulitzer or other prizes for academic administrators. The many faculty members who have won such prizes and other distinctions should realize that the people who recruited the faculty (including the prize winners), administered the budgets, provided the research libraries and computer systems, saw that the lights were on and the heating and cooling systems worked, found and admitted qualified students and graduate assistants, and in dozens of other ways helped the faculty to do their work, deserve some credit for their enabling contributions.

To sum up, it turns out that the university in our society is not such an ivory tower, after all. It has all the problems and foolishness, all the broad vision and narrow-minded shortsightedness, all the integrity and perfidy of what is, for some reason, called the real world. I am prepared to argue that the university is as real as any other part of our world. Its mission as conservator, generator, and purveyor of knowledge may be superior in value to the mission of most other human organizations, but it can suffer from the same human failings as any other human enterprise. Those who affect sophistication may label broad concepts of the nature and mission of a university as naive idealism, but if idealism is not appropriate for universities, where can it exist? Without some measure of idealism, we would live in a very bleak world indeed. The best administrator will keep his or her eyes open to the sometimes disappointing realities inherent in any human endeavor, but will remain firmly grounded in an ideal vision of what a university can and ought to be. Trust everybody, cut the cards, then deal them, ante up, and see what kind of hand you have been given. Often enough it will be a good one, if you can just stay in the game. But then, of course, this is not a game. This is serious. Society, and our students, need administrators who will play their hands well.

Bryant's Laws

Of Academic Administration

1. No one should have an administrative position who wants it. (Chapter 1)

2. Always be aware that a university has no memory and no conscience. (Chapter 1)

3. In searching for an administrator, what you find depends a great deal on what you are looking for, how you look for it, and who is doing the looking. (Chapter 2)

4. A new administrator must experience a full year's cycle of events before being completely familiar with the operations of the unit. (Chapter 3)

5. Never handle the same piece of paper twice. (Chapter 3)

6. Never send a letter or memo written in anger. (Chapter 3)

7. Look carefully at every piece of paper that goes out of your office over your signature. (Chapter 3)

8. If a rule should not apply to you, it probably should not apply to anyone else. (Chapter 3)

9. Trust everybody, but cut the cards (courtesy of Finley Peter Dunne's Mr. Dooley). (Chapter 4)

10. It is easier to work with faculty who act like prima donnas if they sing like prima donnas. (Chapter 5)

11. Stay open to "new" ideas, even when they are old, because the world does change. (Chapter 5)

12. University governance, whether by administrator, faculty council, or committee, has to include decisions and action, not endless theoretical analysis. (Chapter 5)

13. Publication is the usual basis for evaluating research and creative activity, but merely counting titles is not enough. (Chapter 6)

14. Beware of student evaluations in which showmanship trumps intellectual content. (Chapter 6)

15. Research grants should primarily serve the interests of the research, not the researcher or the grantor. (Chapter 7)

16. No academic unit ever thinks it has enough resources. (Chapter 7)

17. When you are told how big a piece of the resources pie your unit is getting, try to find out where the rest of the pie is going and why. (Chapter 7)

18. Democracy is the ideal in governance, but it is important to keep clear what exactly constitutes, or should constitute, the demos. (Chapter 9)

For Students

1. When you go to the spring for water, how much water you bring back depends a whole lot on how big a bucket you take with you. (Chapter 6)

2. Students are not "customers," but rather they are beneficiaries of society who owe society their best efforts to learn. (Chapter 6)

3. When evaluating a course, consider not how much you were entertained, but how much you learned. (Chapter 6)

INDEX